Here's what people are saying about A

"With fresh illustrations, gripping quotati
tics, and practical, hands-on application, Julie B:
source Christian women have needed for a long
seasoned women's ministries director, a teacher,
an aspiring young woman who wants to please God with her gifts, time, and
energy, you will find insightful helps on everything from communication
skills to time management to stress relievers to inspirational stories in *A
Pebble in the Pond*. Julie Baker is a servant leader who models the principles
she teaches. Don't miss this outstanding book. It will change your life and
make you a better leader."

Carol Kent
President, Speak Up Speaker Services, and
author of *Becoming a Woman of Influence*

"Julie is a leader who is willing, even eager, to share her skills and
wisdom with others. Vibrant and engaging on the platform, she transfers her
warmth onto the printed page. In this book she gives clear and practical advice on how we can make our lives that *Pebble in the Pond* that keeps
spreading out to the benefit of all who wish to make the most of their lives."

Florence Littauer
Author, speaker, and
president of Class Speakers, Inc.

Other TimeOut! for Women books by Julie Baker

Time Out for Holiness at Home

Time Out for Holiness at Work

Time Out for Prayer

A Pebble in the Pond
The Ripple Effect

Leadership Skills Every Woman Can Achieve

Julie Baker

For Her. For God. For Real.
faithfulwoman.com

Faithful Woman is an imprint of
Cook Communications Ministries, Colorado Springs, Colorado 80918
Cook Communications, Paris, Ontario
Kingsway Communications, Eastbourne, England

A PEBBLE IN THE POND
© 2001 by Julie Baker

First Printing, 2001
Printed in the United States of America

1 2 3 4 5 6 7 8 9 10 Printing/Year 05 04 03 02 01

Coauthor and Editor: Deb Mendenhall
Cover Design: Jeff Lane
Interior Design: Anita M. Cook

Library of Congress Cataloging-in-Publication Data

Baker, Julie
    A pebble in the pond : the ripple effect / Julie Baker.
        p.cm.
    ISBN 0-7814-3452-1
    1. Christian women--Religious life. 2. Leadership--Religious aspects--Christianity. I. Title.

BV4527 .B332 2000
248.8'43--dc21

00-046226

*May others soon benefit from the ripples your influence
extends as you cast your pebble in the pond*

Contents

Acknowledgments

I so appreciate the many women who have generously shared their ideas about leadership with me and allowed me to pass those insights on to you. These women have participated in our TimeOut for Women! conferences over the past few years. God has used them mightily in women's lives. Now, let me introduce the contributors:

Barbie Cooper, director of Woman Life Ministries at Mount Paran Church of God, Atlanta, Georgia

Liz Curtis Higgs, humorist, radio personality, and author of *Bad Girls of the Bible, One Size Fits All, Mixed Signals*, and many other books

Carol Kent, president of Speak Up Speaker Services, author of *Becoming a Woman of Influence, Tame Your Fears, Mothers Have Angel Wings*, and many other books

Robin Horder-Koop, vice president, North American Business Region Customer Service and Distribution for Amway Corporation

Millie Dienert, Bible teacher and former prayer chairman for the Billy Graham Crusades

Florence Littauer, founder of CLASS, humorist, and author of *Personality Plus, Freeing Your Mind from Memories that Bind, Raising the Curtain on Raising Children,* and many other books

Madeline Manning Mims, Olympic gold medalist, songwriter, and chaplain for the 2000 Olympics in Sydney, Australia

Elisa Morgan, president of MOPS (Mothers of Preschoolers), radio personality of "MomSense," contributing editor to *Christian Parenting Today*, and author of numerous books including *Meditations for Mothers, What Every Mom Needs,* and *What Every Marriage Needs*

Judy Schreur, humorist, motivational speaker, and author of *When Prince Charming Falls off His Horse* and *Creative Grandparenting*

Kay DeKalb Smith, comedic Christian communicator described as the "Carol Burnett of Christian comedy"

Babbie Mason, Word Records song writer, recording artist, and author

Introduction
The Ripple Effect

*Our deeds are like a stone cast into the pool of time.
Though they themselves disappear, their ripples extend to eternity.*
Author Unknown

It's not a new thought: "The hand that rocks the cradle rules the world." Then there's my favorite old axiom, "If momma ain't happy, ain't nobody happy!"

These catchy little phrases resonate with us because the sentiment behind them is universally true: women influence and impact the world.

Our roles as wives, mothers, daughters, sisters, and—for some of us—professionals provide ready-made platforms with tremendous potential for power and influence. Even in cultures where women are not educated, allowed a political voice, or able to enjoy financial independence, mothers have always had sway over their children.

Our deeds, attitudes, and philosophies extend from us to our kids, from our kids to their school, from their school into the workplace, from the workplace into politics and from politics eventually into a global sphere. Our ripples have the potential to influence dozens, hundreds, and even thousands of others.

Simply stated, influence is leadership.

Each time we communicate, we are leading. Every time we make a decision, we are leading. Every time we initiate a change, we are leading. Each one of our actions will bring about a reaction whether it is in the nursery, the school, the church, or the boardroom. It has been said that in her lifetime, even a recluse will impact the lives of over ten thousand people.

The question is, what kind of ripples are we sending? Are we catalysts for positive change or are we harbingers of negativity?

As the philosopher Rowland once said, "Every life we touch is a field, everything we do and all the words we speak are seed. What will the harvest be?"[1]

When I ponder the enormous potential we have to impact another life, the often-told story of Teddy Stallard comes to mind. Teddy was a little boy who certainly could have qualified as "one of the least of these."

Teddy was openly disinterested in school, wore musty, wrinkled clothes, and his uncombed hair looked like a thatch of dry weeds. When his teacher, Miss Thompson, spoke to him, Teddy answered in monosyllables and looked at her with an expressionless, unfocused stare. Unattractive, unmotivated, and distant, Teddy was just plain hard to like.

Miss Thompson always said she loved each student, but one would have to wonder if she actually included Teddy. She seemed to take a perverse delight in writing large, red Xs next to the wrong answers on Teddy's papers, and when there was an F to be put at the top, Miss Thompson's penmanship manifested a distinctive flair. She should have known better; she had Teddy's records, and the pain he was living with was there for all to see. The records read:

1st Grade: Teddy shows promise with his work and attitude, but poor home situation.

2nd Grade: Teddy could do better. Mother is seriously ill. He receives little help at home.

3rd Grade: Teddy is a good boy, but too serious. He is a slow learner. His mother died this year.

4th Grade: Teddy is very slow, but well-behaved. His father shows no interest.

Teddy was a little boy who was slowly being nudged to the periphery of life.

Fall faded into winter with Teddy showing no improvement. When the class had a Christmas party the children took turns adding presents they had brought for Miss Thompson to the growing pile on her desk. The students crowded around the mountain of gifts oohing and aahing as Miss Thompson opened each one. She worked her way to the middle of the pile and pulled out a ragtag present awkwardly wrapped in brown paper and held together with long strings of tape. It was from Teddy Stallard. She was surprised that he had brought her a gift, but he had. On the paper he had scrawled in a childish hand, "For Miss Thompson from Teddy."

Miss Thompson pried open one misshapen corner and out fell a gaudy rhinestone bracelet with half the stones missing and an obviously used bottle of cheap perfume. The other boys and girls began to giggle, but Miss Thompson silenced them by immediately putting on the bracelet and splashing a little of the perfume on her wrist. Holding her wrist up for the other children to smell she said, "Doesn't it smell lovely?" And the children, taking their cue from the teacher, readily agreed with a chorus of "uuummm."

When the students were dismissed for the day, Teddy lingered behind. He slowly walked to her desk and said softly, "Miss Thompson . . . Miss Thompson, you smell just like my mother . . . and her bracelet looks real pretty on you too. I'm glad you liked my presents."

The teacher's heart was pierced. When Teddy left, a humbled Miss Thompson got down on her knees and asked God to forgive her.

The next day when the children came to school, they were welcomed by a new teacher. Although she looked the same, something inside Miss Thompson's heart had transformed her from a teacher into an agent of God. She was now committed to truly loving all her children and showing them in ways that would live on well after they moved to another classroom. She generously gave to all her students, but gave extra attention to the slow ones, especially Teddy Stallard. Miss Thompson proved to be a wonderful leader for Teddy. By the end of the school year Teddy showed dramatic improvement. He had caught up with most of the students and was even ahead of some.

Miss Thompson didn't hear from Teddy for a long time. Then one day, she received a note that read:

> Dear Miss Thompson,
>
> I wanted you to be the first to know I will be graduating second in my class.
>
> Love,
> Teddy Stallard

Four years later, another note came:

> Dear Miss Thompson,
>
> They just told me I will be graduating first in my class.
> I wanted you to be the first to know.
> The university has not been easy, but I liked it.
>
> Love,
> Teddy Stallard

And four years later:

> Dear Miss Thompson:
>
> As of today, I am Theodore Stallard, M.D. How about that? I wanted you to be the first to know. I am getting married next month, the 27th to be exact. I want you to come and sit where my mother would sit if she were alive. You are the only family I have now;
> Dad died last year.
>
> Love,
> Teddy Stallard

Miss Thompson went to that wedding and sat where Teddy's mother would have sat. She deserved to sit there. When he had no one to count on and seemingly few options, Miss Thompson became a leader for Teddy, laying out before him a course for success that he followed all his life. The ripple Miss Thompson cast all those years before was felt not only by Teddy, but by countless others he touched, including the numerous patients who benefited from treatment by a learned doctor who might never have been.

Any of us could be a Miss Thompson in the life of another.

By developing to the best of our abilities the talents and skills God has entrusted to us, we can become leaders who cast positive ripples into the world that will glorify Him.

This book is written for you: the woman who wants to fully develop the leadership potential you already possess, polish the considerable talents you already have but may not even be aware of, and who wants to learn brand-spanking-new skills.

Within these pages, you will discover how to make the best use of your time, handle stress, deal with problemsolving, find balance, and hone communication skills so that others will happily follow. And most importantly, as your skills begin to strengthen, you will discover that in order to lead, you must also learn to follow . . . Jesus Christ, that is.

These teachings are founded upon the Holy Bible. We will walk through its pages and examine some of the biblical models for leadership with Jesus Christ as our ultimate example.

If you've not yet discovered your life purposes or set goals to accomplish them, this can be a life-changing experience. Those who already possess a sense of purpose may find that the information within these pages can be a springboard for greater things such as peace, focus, and a contentment in learning who they are in Jesus Christ.

My prayer for you is:

Heavenly Father, bless Your daughter as she absorbs Your truth in this book. Give her the discernment to know who she is in You, then encourage her as she takes steps to fulfill the potential You've given to her. Give her confidence in You, Lord, that when she is weak, You are strong, that You will never leave her nor forsake her. May each life she touches be a fragrant sacrifice of praise to You with ripples extending to eternity.

Want to Admire a Gifted Woman?
Take a Look in the Mirror

I had just finished speaking on the topic of goal setting and "Letting the Dream Begin" when she began to thread through the laughing, chatting women who lingered after the TimeOut for Women! leadership seminar. She was a stark contrast to those around her. Tears streamed down a face fraught with anguish, and her shoulders hunched against the world as if one more burden might crush them entirely.

When she reached me, the words spilled from her in a torrent. "I don't even know who I am anymore," she whispered. "I've spent my whole life doing the things my husband and children wanted me to do. I don't know if anything interests me. I don't even know what my talents or gifts are and I have no dream."

Does she sound like you?

We women sometimes become so entwined in the lives of others that we lose sight of ourselves. We are magnets for responsibility with task loads that likely include—but are not limited to—managing schedules, arranging activities, balancing a household budget, helping our children realize their potentials, encouraging our husbands in their careers, all the while managing the day-to-day necessities of making sure everyone eats balanced meals, the dog enjoys his walk, and the garbage gets taken out.

Perhaps this doesn't seem much like the portrait of an ideal leader to you, but that woman is a skillful administrator. Just consider the talents necessary to manage a home, raise children, be a partner in a marriage, and be a person worthy of being called a friend. Peel back the veneer of any woman's seemingly ordinary life and you will find many skills necessary for a successful leader.

You see, God has given each of us special talents and gifts that make us as unique from our sisters as one snowflake is from another. Some gifts are spiritual, others are natural, and the mix is different unto each one. Our obligation is to discover that which makes us special. We then need to polish and shine our gifts so that we may be equipped to serve wherever God places us to lead, whether that is in the home, the business world, a ministry, the arts, or as a proprietor, a volunteer, an athlete.

It's just that somewhere along the journey, it's not uncommon for many of us to lose sight of our gifts. As we focus on others, the precious dreams we held for ourselves sometimes become as faded and brittle as a stack of old newspapers full of yesterday's news and expired offers. But fear not. Just because you don't recognize your gifts doesn't mean they aren't there. Even though you might have forgotten your dream, you can rediscover it. Perhaps responsibilities came so fast that you didn't have time to develop a dream of your own. Take comfort in the fact that regardless of your age or current circumstance, you can find it for the very first time.

God will help each of us to recognize the gifts He has given, reveal our dreams, and empower us in the equipping process; we only need ask Him. I've created an acronym to help demonstrate the four foundational steps that serve to guide you and put you on the path to realizing your potential in Him. Come with me as we do some SOUL searching. As Christian women, we are to:

Seek God

Obey Him

Understand His Word

Love others

Let's look at some of the things God has said about SOUL searching:

Seek

"I [God] love those who love me, and those who seek me find me" (Prov. 8:17). Yes, some among us have had a "Damascus Road" experience, but many have had to search for God. Consider the wise men who sought God by following the star He provided. Yes, He stands at our heart's door and knocks, but He doesn't barge in and break it down for us; we must open the door and ask Him to enter (Rev. 3:20). When we seek Him, He will be found.

Obey

"If anyone loves me, he will obey my teaching" (John 14:23). Although salvation is a free gift, we have a responsibility through obedient behavior to show our devotion to Christ. His teachings are intended to protect us. Obeying is both for His benefit: we worship Him through obedience; and for our benefit: we enjoy His protection.

Understand

"All Scripture is God-breathed and is useful for teaching, rebuking, correcting and training in righteousness, so that the man of God may be thoroughly equipped for every good work" (2 Tim. 3:16). How can we seek Him and obey Him unless we know and understand the Scriptures? This is the place where we meet Him and He is revealed to us. We must be constant seekers and students of Scripture if we want to be equipped to fulfill His purpose for our lives.

Love

When asked what was the most important of the commandments, Jesus answered: "Love the Lord your God with all your heart and with all your soul and with all your mind and with all your strength. The second is this: 'Love your neighbor as yourself'" (Mark 12:30-31).

If you feel shaky on the path you are traveling today, these steps will serve as a compass to direct you back to God. As you grow closer and learn to depend upon Him and pray for His direction, you will be better able to discern the gifts He has given to you and how you may use them for His kingdom.

In each heart He has tucked talents, desires, and dreams. In each life He has scattered opportunities. Our job is to equip ourselves by developing the gifts God has entrusted to us so that we will be ready for service at any time. When we walk in step with the Lord, He places the dreams, the desires, and the determination within us to accomplish His work. The process will be different for each one. Some may realize their purposes immediately. For others, it may take more time.

I have a friend who wants desperately to go to the mission field for a two- to three-year term. She's on fire and ready to go. She wants to pack those bags and head for parts unknown as quickly as possible and do God's work. But not one door has opened to her and she is becoming more and more discouraged. Is the burning in her heart a misplaced desire? Is the mission field not for her? Is she longing after something that is really not right for her?

I don't think so. Her deep yearning for mission work indicates to me that God has infused her heart with passion and given her a dream. So what's wrong? Consider this: she has young children at home, elderly parents who depend upon her, and she is involved in some wonderful causes that need her special touch at this time.

It seems clear to me that this is the wrong season in her life for that dream to be fulfilled. I've encouraged her to enjoy the process as God equips her for the work to come. It is my belief that because God has given her the dream, surely when she is totally prepared, He will open the right doors at the right time. "There is a time for everything, and a season for every activity under heaven" (Ecc. 3:1).

We are not to wait idly for our dreams to be fulfilled, but are to actively work toward our goals by constantly fortifying our skills and talents and knowledge of the Scripture, growing stronger in our walk with God. In the process we must be patient and ever watchful for opportunities.

Noah had to wait about one hundred years from the time God presented His purpose—to build the ark—until the first drop of rain fell. Yet I believe Noah was a man at peace because he understood and obeyed God's instructions to him.

The Power of Passion

I believe we would all merrily trot along after God if we only knew clearly and decisively where He wanted us to go. One of the most difficult aspects of following God is being able to hear the difference between His voice and our own desires that insistently and daily make their preferences known. This issue alone would keep a roomful of theologians talking for months before each goes off to write his or her own book about it. My own feeling is that as we grow more obedient, pray regularly, study the Bible, and deeply seek God, discerning when He is doing the talking becomes easier.

I also believe that one prominent way God gives direction is by setting hearts afire. Think for a moment about your favorite Christian brothers and sisters. In any Christian group you will find these folks: some care deeply about mission fields, others want to make sure the church is administered according to biblical principles, some are absolutely giddy about telling Bible stories to toddlers, and for others, a day without breaking out into song would be as dreary as a California vacation during the rainy season.

That's passion. Sometimes God plants a burning desire deep in a heart. Once infused with passion from the Master, that heart cannot be content unless it is doing that which it loves.

Hockey star Wayne Gretsky is one who understands the power of passion. A born athlete, Gretsky's natural talent skyrocketed him to one of the most visible positions in professional hockey. Upon his retirement, Gretsky choked out heartfelt words of thanks to the fans and thanks to God. My husband and I watched that emotional moment on ESPN, and I wrote down the exact words he shared: "I want to thank God for my talent," he began. He then stopped as if realizing something for the first time. "No," he corrected himself. "I thank God for my passion."

Conversely, lack of passion just might be an indication that you are putting your energies into the wrong area. Our son taught me this principle. He ran cross-country for three years in high school. He always placed in the top three on his team, and often came in first or second in multischool competitions. Running is his natural talent and he is incredible at it even when he is not in training. Just before beginning his senior year, he sheepishly came to his father and me with downcast eyes and made the statement, "I know you guys aren't going to like this or understand, but I've chosen not to run cross this year."

My first instinct was to yell and scream, "What? Not run? Are you crazy? You have potential to be first in all the meets this year and possibly take regionals! And the team needs you!" Instead I bit my tongue and allowed his dad to have the floor. Dad asked, "Why don't you want to run, Son?"

Our son responded: "I don't like it. Never have. Never will."

Like Gretsky our son had the raw talent. But unlike Gretsky, he lacked the passion and the love of the sport.

Sometimes called "heart," passion is that mysterious intangible that gives a person a hefty edge over others who might be more talented or more intelligent but who do not have a burning in their hearts. It's not uncommon to see someone whose passion exceeds his talent do far better than the one loaded in talent, but lacking heart. I have known musicians, athletes, and businesspeople who weren't born with an unusual knack or outstanding talent in their field, but whose passion gave them the drive and stamina to pursue a dream and see it fulfilled. An unbeatable combination is when God puts the gifts of passion and natural talent into the same person. The possibilities are dazzling.

There are others among us to whom God has given incredible dreams, natural talent, and creative abilities. The raw potential to do anything is right there, yet those ideas never make it from their minds to the drawing table and eventually into reality. The pebble just never gets cast into the pond. And some are like the lady who tearfully whispered that she had no dream. The passion has grown so dim that we can't see a flicker of that former flame.

That passion can be reawakened! It's not gone, it's merely sleeping, waiting for us to remember that it's there.

If this is you, go by yourself to a quiet place, sit for a while, and think about what you once loved. Much like the literary technique of foreshadowing in which an author hints in early pages what is to happen later in a book, God will sometimes give us in our childhood a glimpse of His future plans for us. What did you love as a child, as a teenager, as a student and young adult? Ponder each season of your early life as if you were a detective searching out clues. Write them down, pray for discernment, and wait for your heart to leap.

How to Make Dreams Come True

Dreams come in all shapes and sizes. They don't have to take on the magnitude of building an ark, going off to the mission field, or succeeding as a professional athlete. Sometimes a dream is as humble as the desire to cook nutritious meals every day. And sometimes, humble or not, that's just about impossible to do. The question, of course, is why? We have such great intentions, but never seem to be able to accomplish them. How come?

Have you ever considered that a dream is nothing but a pleasant thought unless it has a plan attached to it? A dream will stay just that—a lovely idea—unless you put feet under it.

Give this a try: At your best time of day, sit down with a pad of paper and a pen for a frank assessment. Begin with a prayer for guidance and then think about the obstacles that are keeping you from doing what you really want to do. Move on to the steps you must take to change your life. Write them down. Make a plan to equip yourself to realize your dream.

Make sure you do this at your best time of day. Are you a night person? Go to bed twenty minutes early with pen and paper. Are you a morning person? After breakfast, don't answer the telephone, read the paper, retrieve e-mail, or wash one dish for the first twenty minutes. Consider it your time and guard it jealously.

Be creative as you ponder these things. Let your mind explore every option.

Let's say, for example, that your goal is to read more inspirational, self-help books, but you just can't seem to find the time. Begin by assessing where you spend a lot of time. If being Taxi Mom consumes hours as you shuttle kids from soccer to baseball to ballet, look for another mom who is willing to trade off driving days with you. How about reading books as you eat lunch? Check out books on tape from the library and listen to them while you cook dinner or clean the house.

There aren't many of us who haven't worried at one time or another about making paychecks stretch for the entire week. If you are struggling with this, think about your spending. Do you sometimes make impulsive buys at the supermarket? Do you plan your weekly meals around the items on sale at the grocery store or do you buy convenience foods? Do you eat out more often than you should? Do the kids really need to go to a beauty shop to get their hair cut, or will a barber or one of those low-cost chain beauty shops do?

Is your dream a little bigger? Would you, for example, like to become a teacher? Do you need to begin working toward a college degree in education, or finish one? Do you need to get an extra job to earn the money to further your education? Have you considered applying for a scholarship? Are teachers needed in your area? If not, are you willing to relocate?

Your dream is to sing Christian music professionally. Many people sing well in the shower. Do you truly have the talent? Have you ever sung? Does your choir director think you have the voice to be a soloist? Do you have the passion to devote yourself to a grueling daily rehearsal schedule? Would you be willing to develop an outstanding repertoire? Do you know the steps necessary to prepare a demo recording? Do you know what to do with it once you have one?

You long for a better understanding of God's Word and want to facilitate a home Bible study. Is there someone you can talk to at your church designated to help with home studies? What study books are offered at your local Bible bookstore? Would you invite neighbors, Christians only, the unchurched?

Your dream is to start your own business. Is your idea viable? Is there a market for it? Do you know how to do a market study, or would you hire someone to do that for you? Do you need financial capital? What kind of collateral is necessary for a bank loan?

Your dream is to write. Do you want to write fiction or magazine features? Have you ever written? Have you ever been published? Do you need to take a couple of classes to find out about the business side of writing? Should you enroll in some classes to learn about writing itself? Have you talked to the local newspaper editor about whether she buys freelance feature stories?

Your dream is to somehow organize your crazy house so that most every day there are clean towels, a clutter-free environment, and a nutritious entrée at the evening meal. Beaver Cleaver's mom seemed to be able to do this every day, but in real life this sometimes is the toughest dream of all. Does everything in your home have a place, or are you drowning in clutter? Do you need to send a few bags over to the Salvation Army? Are other family members leaving their stuff all over? Toss their leavings in a basket tucked in the coat closet. This will get it out of sight but keep it readily available to the guilty party who comes looking for it. Is there an older child who can wash a load of towels every week as part of his or her chores? Do you plan meals or try to figure them out on the run? What steps do you need to take to equip yourself to run an efficient home?

When I think of equipping women for service and leadership, I often think of Joshua, the uncomplaining number two guy under Moses for decades. Joshua never competed for the number one slot. He obediently followed Moses' advice. He basked freely in God's presence on Mt. Sinai. He practiced his battle skills until God looked at him one day and confirmed that he was totally equipped to lead. Then He gave Joshua charge over the Children of Israel and he successfully led them into the Promised Land.

What is your Promised Land for this and future seasons of your life? What talents do you need to hone and polish so that when opportunities to serve God present themselves, you will be ready? Are you willing to invest the time, energy, and prayer to make the most of the talents God has given to you? Do you have passion? Are you willing to put your energies into reaching a series of smaller goals that might be necessary before you see the fulfillment of your dream?

Assessment of the problem and a plan of action can turn an insurmountable obstacle into a manageable solution and an unreachable dream into a reality.

Enjoy the Ride!

As you endeavor to equip yourself as a leader for God's service, remember that like life, this process can be very much like a roller-coaster ride.

Some of us sit in the middle car gripping the hand bar, gritting our teeth, and hanging on with white knuckles enduring the ride until it is over. Others fight for the front seat because that is where the thrills are. When propelled to the highest point, we raise our arms above our heads and yell, "Yippee!

Whee!" as the car plummets down that first big drop. We enjoy every dip, valley, climb, and curve and don't want the ride to ever end.

As we move ahead in learning new skills and polishing old favorites until they gleam, we will encounter circumstances that will bring us to those roller-coaster dips, valleys, climbs, curves, and deep, dark tunnels. Some experiences will be difficult, painful, and involve self-sacrifice. But try to enjoy the ride. At the end of those rolling, tumultuous tracks lies a wealth of knowledge born from cresting the sun-kissed hills as well as from enduring dark tunnels. Remember that you are preparing for greater things that are to come. Keep in mind, too, that sometimes the difference between success and failure is simply a matter of persistence. Abraham Lincoln lost at least five elections before he was propelled by popular vote to the highest office in the land.[1]

Examples of people who were empowered by God to persist long after it seemed prudent to do so abound in the Bible. Among them is the Apostle Paul, who recounts hardships he faced in 2 Corinthians 11:23-27:

> I have worked much harder, been in prison more frequently, been flogged more severely, and been exposed to death again and again. Five times I received from the Jews the forty lashes minus one. Three times I was beaten with rods, once I was stoned, three times I was shipwrecked, I spent a night and a day in the open sea, I have been constantly on the move. I have been in danger from rivers, in danger from bandits, in danger from my own countrymen, in danger from Gentiles; in danger in the city, in danger in the country, in danger at sea; and in danger from false brothers. I have labored and toiled and have often gone without sleep; I have known hunger and thirst and have often gone without food. I have been cold and naked.

And during one of those stints in prison, he writes eloquent letters from jail to people in cities he's visited and those he's never been to. He doesn't rot in jail or seethe with anger and frustration. In the midst of persecution he realizes that he can sing praises to the Lord and be "content in any and every situation" (Phil. 4:12). These letters not only trained the new converts of his day, but serve today as our most meaningful instructions in Christian living and doctrine. Paul is one who certainly overcame hardships, fulfilled God's purposes, and saw a dream come true.

Difficult situations can lead us into a deeper understanding of God's love, provision, and plan for our lives. Sometimes our suffering becomes the most valuable element in the equipping process as we gain valuable experience or insight in ways we could never have predicted. Are you willing to let God mold your abilities in this way so that you may glorify Him by providing leadership to others?

Conditioned for Service

The molding and equipping process also involves conditioning. When I think about conditioning, I see my husband, excited and ambitious on his first day as a runner. He pulled on those running shoes and bolted from our driveway onto the pavement with a goal to run down the hill about two-tenths of a mile to the railroad tracks at the end of our street.

His gait on the return trip was considerably slower because he was gasping for air and nursing a cramped hamstring. But he continued, conquering more ground and becoming stronger every day. And now, some fifteen years later, thanks to training and conditioning, he runs three to five miles at a time, up steep hills and against the wind. He has run in numerous races, some as far as fifteen miles in distance. Proper training and conditioning has equipped him to become a successful runner.

In 1 Corinthians 9:24-26, Paul uses the example of a runner to encourage us as we equip ourselves for our eternal destination. "Remember that in a race everyone runs, but only one person gets the prize. You must run in such a way that you will win. . . . So I run straight to the goal with purpose in every step" (NLT).

Are you running toward your goals with purpose in every step? Or are you just allowing life to happen to you as it comes, watching in vain those unfulfilled dreams vaporize before taking shape in your mind or on paper?

Remember that God can use any circumstance to equip and condition you as you run toward your goal. We must, as instructed in James 1, "consider it pure joy . . . whenever [we] face trials of many kinds" (v. 2). Even setbacks can be a part of God's spiritual training program for us as we strive to be equipped for the fulfillment of His plan.

*Dear Father, may Your daughter see clearly those plans,
hopes, and dreams that You have placed within her heart.
Give her the passion and persistence to prepare herself for
service in Your kingdom. Amen.*

two

Every Woman Is a Leader—
Like It or Not

E sther. Mary, the mother of Jesus. Lydia. When you think of these biblical women, doesn't your heart just kinda melt with admiration and respect?

Esther's story, told in the book named for her, reveals to us a woman with monumental leadership qualities. She not only demonstrated that she was a risk taker as she embarked on an act that could have cost her her life, but she ended up foiling Haman's plan to exterminate the Jews. She saved the very nation that would bring forth the Messiah! And, I might add, she did it not with force, but through wisdom, forethought, and perseverance.

Consider Mary, a humble peasant girl whose character exemplified a willingness to obey her God no matter the cost to her reputation. Although she was not a queen as Esther became, think of the influence her life has held for women—mothers especially—for two thousand years. One has only to picture her at the foot of the cross as she painfully watched her Son die, to see her devotion and loyalty to the God-Man who was oft misunderstood, unfairly tortured, and unjustly killed.

The story of Lydia, told in Acts 16, shows us a successful businesswoman who was responsible for a huge household. Her leadership overflowed from her workplace to her homeplace as she insisted that her entire entourage worship the true Messiah.

Perhaps you and I are just a bit intimidated by these women. Or perhaps we look at their lives, influence, and reputation and are inspired to try a bit harder to be just a little more like them.

Are these women much different from you and me? I would venture to presume that each of them was just as vulnerable, insecure, and confused as we are at times. However, because they put their faith in God, He was able to work in and through them to change not just the nations they lived among, but the world for eternity.

They responded in obedience to God's instructions. They willingly submitted to Him and took advantage of the opportunities He spread before them. They gathered courage for their assignments not from their own resources, but from God alone. They were ordinary, just like us, yet through faith, they accomplished extraordinary things because they clearly saw what God was asking of them. "But the plans of the Lord stand firm forever, the purposes of his heart through all generations" (Ps. 33:11). These women were incredible leaders not because of a leadership title or position, but because they put their faith in God.

Whether we know it or not, whether we like it or not, we also lead. Some of us are already in a leadership role similar to Lydia looking for good information as to how we can be more effective in leading our coworkers and household. Some of us see ourselves as "wanna-be" leaders. Perhaps we have more in common with Esther, who learned much about influence from her family and life experience. We are open for helpful guidance so that we can confidently accept and provide leadership when the opportunities arise.

Yet others of us are like young Mary, standing at the crossroads of a decision. We can either accept it and trust in the Lord, or we can be afraid of leadership because it appears too lofty or too frightening an assignment.

No matter the category you seem to fit in at the moment, God is ready to help you lead and guide those within your sphere of influence. Are we willing to comply and prepare? If so, God has tremendous blessings in store.

So, What's Stopping You?

If you are reluctant to expand your leadership skills and pursue your dreams, it may be that you harbor some fears or because you feel that you lack the necessary skills. If so, you're in good company. Many of us share these fears and recognize our need to improve our leadership skills.

First let's take a moment to list and analyze typical fears that every leader with a dream shares, and consider how these fears may actually become positive springboards to developing stronger leadership characteristics. Then we will take a look at the leadership qualities you already possess that we will later build upon.

Fear of Failure

Have you ever heard the term "paralyzed by fear"? It suggests that fear is an entity so powerful that it makes movement impossible. Fear of failure can keep even the most talented individuals from reaching their potentials or realizing a dream. Why do we fear failure? What's so bad about it? Perhaps we need to look at failure from a new and positive perspective.

Let's face it, every person has endeavors that fail. Why fear a fact of life? Each leader experiences times when she feels that she has truly blown it. But that does not mean that she, the leader, is a failure.

It could be assumed that Thomas Edison had hundreds of experiments that failed, since his inventions were not perfected without many attempts. Yet look at the outcome of his "failures" by considering all of the successes that ensued. We would not consider the lightbulb a failure, yet at first it probably did not resemble the lightbulb we enjoy today.

Had he given in to the paralyzing fear of failure, he might never have proceeded in what, frankly, must have appeared as bizarre behavior! He must have arrived at the correct conclusion that failure is inevitable, but can and does lead to positive results.

The fear of failure can serve to protect a project when it is channeled into the planning stages. This healthy fear forces us to take a critical look at the plan or circumstance and consider all of the scenarios—all of the possible ways that it could fail. As we discover those, we have the opportunity to correct the problem and move on to a successful completion. As has been said, "Success is never final and failure never fatal."

Fear of Making Mistakes

Unless something has recently changed, my understanding is that only Jesus is perfect. That means that all of us are going to make mistakes. The issue with mistakes is, when we make them, as we will, how will we handle them?

The first instinct many of us have is to pass the buck and use a scapegoat or make an excuse. Good leaders, however, admit their mistakes, take full responsibility, and then they move on. Just as we do from failures, we can learn a great deal from our mistakes. The only mistake with mistakes is if we repeat them or don't learn from them.

Fear of Risk Taking

The old axiom "nothing ventured, nothing gained" is quite true. A healthy degree of risk is necessary for the success of any endeavor. Why do we fear taking a risk? Is it because we are afraid of failing or making a mistake? While it's true that we may lose something, it is also true that we have much to gain.

In *Leading Without Power*, Max DuPree encourages healthy risk taking and says, "By avoiding risk we really risk what's most important in life—reaching toward growth, our potential, and a true contribution to a common good. . . . To risk nothing is perhaps the greatest risk of all."[1] Risk taking may be the very thing that propels us to accomplish our potentials.

Fear of Not Being Liked

Here's a biggie for women. Most of us want desperately to be liked and accepted, so the fear of not being liked may keep us from taking on leadership responsibilities. While it's true that a leader may sometimes have to make unpopular decisions or can't please everybody, more likely than not, a majority of people will support her efforts. We're never going to hit 100 percent on any level. I like how Zig Ziglar puts it: "Don't be distracted by criticism. Remember—the only taste of success some people have is when they take a bite out of you."[2]

During a Sunday School lesson my husband was teaching, he asked a volunteer to come up to the front of the classroom and handed him a glass filled with water. Then, without warning, my husband took the volunteer's arm and began to jostle it until water spilled all over. He turned to the class and asked, "Why did water spill out of the cup?" Duh. "You shook his arm."

"Not really." He explained: "Water came out of the cup because water was in the cup." It's important to remember that people overflow with whatever is in them. If they harbor resentment, bitterness, and a critical spirit, when shaken a little, that's what's going to spill out. If we happen to be the one to shake them a little, we may get splattered with what they spill on us. It may appear that they dislike us, when the reality is that they are dealing with deep inner struggles that cause them to lash out in anger.

Of course, we cannot always be liked by everyone—a reality that we are going to have to accept. It certainly hurts, but if we are convinced that we are headed in the right direction, with God's help, we can stay true to the course whether we feel liked or not.

Fear of Change

Many of us are comfortable with the familiar and enjoy keeping the status quo—even when it keeps us from going anywhere. In order to fulfill a dream, we may have to make small to radical changes. Venturing into the unknown is sometimes frightening. Maybe we fear change because it won't be embraced by those around us who fear change. Maybe it makes us feel uncomfortable. Or maybe it threatens our control. One way to combat fear of change is to live in a constant attitude of continuous improvement where we evaluate often the effectiveness of our work. If it is not helping us fulfill our dream, we recognize this and make necessary changes that allow our goals to be met.

We cannot become what we hope to by remaining where we are.

Fear of Overcommitment

All of us are allotted the same twenty-four hours in a day, so we must take inventory of how we spend our time and why. The fear of overcommitment is a healthy fear that allows us to take a realistic look at how much we can really accomplish and still perform up to our ability.

However, the fear of overcommitment has kept many women from finishing a college degree, accepting a promotion, enjoying a ceramics class, or joining a Bible study. It also can keep us from considering additional responsibility that could prove very beneficial to us and our sphere of influence. We will explore later how personal goal setting and effective time management skills may allow for a dream to be realized without overcommitment.

Fear of Success

Did you do a double take? This is not a typo. I've had countless students and colleagues who are so afraid of being successful that they almost sabotage their own efforts, sometimes unconsciously.

We have a friend who is a successful psychologist with a thriving practice. He was the first in his family to receive a college degree, which in itself made him feel uncomfortable . . . fearing family jealousy or criticism. Then, when he received his doctorate, he seriously considered moving across the country so that he didn't have to be "ashamed" of his success before his family and friends.

Our own son, running cross-country, came in first at his first meet, then never did it again. He didn't like the responsibility of being number one, and didn't enjoy the attention it gave to him. He didn't want to be looked to as the only one responsible for winning every race because it would take an incredible amount of additional training and stamina to stay at the number one position.

I've heard it said that it takes more work for a recording artist to stay at the top of the charts than it does to get there the first time. Success brings with it a responsibility that takes focus and consistency to maintain. The dread of this keeps many from ever mounting the next step on the staircase to leadership.

Whether a person feels unworthy of success, or unwilling to work hard enough to stay successful, the best thing we can do with any of our successful ventures is to give the glory to God. God has given us certain abilities and talents and expects us to use them, not so that we should boast, but so that we can point to His miracles in our lives. In John 14:13 Jesus tells His disciples that they can ask anything in His name and He will do it. Why? "So that the Son may bring glory to the Father." Isn't it amazing that though He Himself was God incarnate, He wanted all of the praise to go to His Father? Successful leaders give God the glory for their success.

If one or some of these fears are keeping you from pursuing your dreams and attaining your God-ordained goals, be encouraged that everyone who steps out of her comfort zone to fulfill a dream struggles, to a degree, with the same fears. However, as Christians, we have been given a Comforter who loves us so much that He has offered to take away our fears.

In almost every biblical account where God sent a message via angel or through a vision, the first thing the messenger said was "Fear not." This is still God's message to us today. Do not fear the possibility of failure, making mistakes, being criticized, or attaining success. Don't let those fears act as a barrier between you and the accomplishment of God's purpose for you.

It takes faith to step out, but this is what God asks of us. When Peter stepped out of the boat to walk on the water toward Jesus, he demonstrated a huge step of faith (Matt.14:28-31). And he continued to walk on the water until the wind frightened him. It was his fear and doubt that caused him to begin sinking. Just then, Jesus reached out His hand and caught him. So it is with us.

You Already Are a Leader

Women, because of their nature and instincts, display incredible leadership qualities. I've often maintained that the best thing to happen in recent years is the addition of leadership positions for women in the corporate world and church arenas. Women bring to the attention of an organization valuable aspects that might otherwise be overlooked.

Just look at the sought-after leadership qualities you probably already possess:

Sensitivity

Many women are naturally sensitive. Sensitivity involves being ready to respond and many women by nature are responders. Sensitivity has been compared to a radio transmission being picked up by a sensitive radio receiver. Women are very good at picking up signals. Sensitivity is a positive and necessary quality for a successful leader.

Compassion

Many women have natural compassion. In Mark 8:2, Jesus, teaching the multitudes, remarked, "I have compassion for these people; they have already been with me three days and have nothing to eat." Without compassion for others, a leader becomes cold, distant, arrogant, and self-serving. Women often bring a warmth and compassion to leadership that enhances their environment. As Bob Briner states, "The kind of leader who produces lasting, positive results, particularly that last for eternity, will have compassion."[3] Without compassion, an organization has no heart.

Identify and Encourage Potential

Many women have the innate ability to bring out potential in others. One only needs to picture a mom coaxing her eleven month old to take another step or hearing her yell "Jump!" to her eleven year old on the diving board to understand how a woman can see potential in others. Women have a wonderful way of seeing inner qualities in others and encouraging them to act on them. It's an "I know you can do it" attitude. Perhaps this is why in Titus 2 Paul knew the success older women would enjoy as they taught the younger women. We often see inner qualities that a good mentor brings to the surface. The best leaders are those who see potential and encourage others to develop it.

A Crack Juggler

Many women are naturally good at time management and possess strong organizational skills. Most of us are thrown into a big circus ring that requires us to juggle a multitude of roles and responsibilities—sometimes all at the same time! We come home from work and throw in a load of laundry before dropping off our son at baseball, run a couple of errands, start the meat for dinner, pick up our son and bring him home, toss the laundry into the dryer, and continue cooking dinner, after which we fold the laundry and set the table. Good leaders know how to work on multiple tasks at the same time, keeping their focus on obtaining several goals at one time.

Knowing How to Affirm Others

Women certainly know the importance of noticing and commenting on a friend's new haircut, dress, or lipstick color. While these may seem like small things to compliment or insignificant items to notice, it points out that women know there is value in giving positive affirmation. And it works. By affirming others, a leader provides the inner confidence that gives another person needed encouragement to explore and excel in new areas.

Willingness to Listen

At home or in the workplace, we have discovered the importance of listening. How many times have some of us—because we've listened to our child—diagnosed correctly her condition long before the doctor is convinced? How many times have we listened to opposing opinions on a work-related topic and come to the solution first—just because we listened with sensitivity and compassion? All successful leaders have learned how to listen with empathy that is results-oriented.

Desire to Do Her Best

My experience is that women desire to give their best ideas and provide their best effort so that any endeavor they are involved in is successful. Sometimes we do this sacrificially and without thought of receiving praise in return. This is the essence of what is termed "servant leadership." As a leader provides her best, she challenges others to walk in her footsteps and put their best foot forward.

Intuition

The dictionary defines intuition as "a truth or revelation arrived at by insight."[4] When researching all the facts and collecting all the data leads to no conclusive decision, a woman's insight often brings a decisive spirit to her environment. One of the greatest strengths any leader brings to an organization is the ability to make a decision.

Effective Communication Skills

Not too many of us have failed Telephone Talking 101 or Conversation over Lunch 400. Women have long been noted as the more verbal of the sexes, which is one of the greatest assets a leader can display. Here's why: Even the most brilliant of ideas must be clearly articulated so that others catch the vision. Our words make others "see" things the way they can be. If we cannot communicate our vision, the idea is dead in its tracks and we can never take a single step forward. However, if we can passionately explain the vision and motivate others so they "see" it, we have demonstrated successful leadership.

What's Your Mission?

If you are a baby boomer, you may remember, as I do, watching the original television series called "Mission Impossible." The beginning teaser always zeroed in on the show's leading character listening to his instructions on a small tape recorder. After the assignment was described, the voice on the recording would say, "And this mission—should you decide to accept it . . ." and after a few more details, the tape recorder would go up in smoke.

As we've already discussed, each woman who has committed her life to Jesus Christ has talents and skills she can develop to fulfill any opportunity God gives her. Her relationship with Jesus Christ propels her into adventures that fulfill those opportunities. These adventures become her mission. Mission means "the sending of an individual or group by an AUTHORITY to perform specific service."[5] Isn't that beautifully clear? God is our authority who sends us on a mission to perform His service. And with God, no mission is impossible!

A mission statement is a necessary first step. It helps you to state your purpose or goals and articulate the vision you see. Before we can even discuss leadership skill development, it's imperative for you to clearly write out your personal mission statement. In essence, it articulates on paper what you understand your purpose is as a daughter of Jesus Christ. Once this is clear, you will measure your priorities, the proper way to spend your time, the handling of stress, making decisions, and developing communication skills against your personal mission statement.

Simply defined, a mission statement articulates a desired outcome or result. It is the outward expression of your inner vision, much like an architect's initial blueprint. Your mission statement should:

- Be clear, concise, and easily understood
- Correctly represent your vision and heart

- Be repeated and referred to often

- Keep you focused and on track

- Be referenced when making decisions

- Help define your purpose

- Be reevaluated from time to time

Frequent TimeOut speaker and author Carol Kent has a personal mission statement that includes the idea of "reproducing herself." What she means is that she wants to teach others techniques for sharing their testimony through effective communication skills. Any skill that she has mastered, she willingly shares with others, in hopes that they will become proficient as well.

We have, from time to time, reevaluated the TimeOut for Women! mission statement and considered changing the wording, but ended up returning to the original, which is: "To encourage and inspire women of all denominations in their spiritual journey and bring non-Christians to a saving knowledge of Jesus Christ."

Every decision, activity, and conversation within our organization takes into account this mission statement. As new ideas are considered for implementation, we always ask ourselves, "Will this minister?" If it will, we research felt needs, deadlines, and budgets. If the idea does not underscore the mission statement, we set it aside.

My own personal mission statement has evolved over the years. When I was teaching in a secular high school, my mission focused on how my life could impact my students. When I was a full-time stay-at-home mom, my priority was my home and family. Now that I am singing, speaking, and teaching to mostly women, my personal mission statement reflects just that: "To use my musical and teaching talents in encouraging women to realize their God-given potentials, bring them to a more intimate understanding of Jesus Christ, and assist them in honoring their leadership skills." Everything in my personal mission statement underscores the mission statement of the organization I serve. Not all will be so fortunate, but don't let that discourage you from articulating exactly what you feel your personal mission is.

Developing a mission statement can be a very healthy, introspective exercise for each of us as we put it on paper. Can you articulate your goals and ambitions and describe the avenues that will take you there? Spend some time in prayer, take inventory of your dreams and talents, then try to come up with a one-sentence personal mission statement. This exercise could be an exciting turning point in your life.

What's Your Vision?

"Good leaders have vision; better leaders share a vision; the best leaders invite others in spreading this vision."[6] I've heard it said that only 10 to 20 percent of people think in visions, so perhaps this is a confusing idea to understand. In simple terms, a visionary is someone who sees clearly the whole picture. Because of this, she has a responsibility to help others who may not be visionary to understand and accept the whole picture.

A vision is much like the blueprint for the construction of a building. The idea for the architecture begins in the mind of the designer. She has to somehow convey what is in her mind to the construction crew so that they can also see her plan. She visualizes the foundation posts, the basement, the framing in of the rooms, the roofing, electrical wiring, plumbing, and fixtures. She creates in her mind all aspects of the details—both inside and out. As all of these ideas are displayed on the blueprint she provides to the workers, they too begin to see her ideas and know what their part is in making the dream a reality.

What happens if the vision is delayed or not communicated? A group of people are in the jungle hacking away with their machetes, aimlessly forging ahead. Eventually, the leader climbs a tree and sees the whole landscape and yells back, "Hey, we're in the wrong jungle!" Providing vision ensures that each person understands the mission, the goal, and the desired final outcome so that all efforts can be focused on obtaining that end. When those are in place, everyone will end up in the right jungle.

Many years ago we were invited to a reception at the home of Pat and Deedee Robertson of the "700 Club." It was so interesting to listen to their vision for an organization that would impact the tragedy of worldwide hunger. Pat clearly outlined to us the countries that they could help and how Americans could be involved in so noble a cause. Then it was just a vision; today it is a reality in Operation Blessing. It began as a vision and became a mission.

Before we cast a vision, we should develop skills that enable us to clearly define our purpose and express it in a mission statement.

Before moving on to the following chapters, which will explore ways to improve your leadership skills, take a moment to develop a clear personal mission statement based upon your purpose and vision.

Father, we come humbly before You today asking You to take away the fears that may be keeping us from fulfilling Your purposes in our lives. Lord, I ask that You reveal Your plans and purposes in my sister's life so that she has a clear vision of her mission. Then, Lord, give her wisdom and courage to follow You until her task is done and she has completed her mission. Amen.

My Personal Mission Statement

_____

_____

_____

_____

Date: _____

three

Huh?
Did You Say Something?

Even the most violent critic will frequently soften and be subdued
in the presence of a patient, sympathetic listener.[1]

You might think that listening is a passive activity that requires little of us and has even less to do with leadership. However, in the world of successful leaders, nothing could be further from the truth. Effective listening skills enable us to glean valuable information, can lead to wisdom, and yes, might even deliver power. Listening with the head and the heart may be the single most valuable asset a leader can have. Perhaps you've never looked at it this way, but as Dale Carnegie suggests, effective listening can even allow a leader to exert control.

Look at the control that Christ maintained through effective listening skills during a very sticky situation in John 8:4-11. The religious leaders were trying to trap Him into going against the Law of Moses. They brought to Him a woman who was caught in the act of adultery, demanding that she be stoned, as was the Mosaic Law. Some have surmised that even the "catch" was a setup to use this woman as a pawn in their game to discredit Jesus.

Notice that no matter what they say, accuse, or question, Jesus stays silent. Interestingly, He seems to go against some examples of effective listening that we will focus on in this study; but He does so in order to successfully diffuse a potentially deadly situation. He does not make eye contact after a certain point. In fact, He seems to almost remove Himself emotionally and physically from the situation by bending down and writing in the sand. Both times that He listens He stoops down.

Since the accused woman remained standing and He stooped, Jesus allowed Himself to be placed in a position of servanthood to her. His silence allowed the group of accusers enough time to impatiently state and restate their case, hungry for Jesus to hang Himself on this one. Jesus lets them vent until they don't have anything left to say and are so curious as to how He will respond that they become quiet.

Each time Jesus responds to them with words, the Bible says that He straightened up. He bent to listen, stood to speak. He carefully selects a few choice words, then speaks to them from a position of authority—both physically and spiritually.

His verbal constraint allowed the Pharisees to know they had been heard and understood so that He could retort with His wise words—and He speaks to them only *when* He knew they were finally ready to listen to His response. Had He lashed out immediately, been defensive, or not heard them out, it could have incited a riot.

So what happened? Finish the story. Instead . . .

When and how to listen, and the appropriate ways to respond, require discernment, forethought, and training. My prayer for you is that your personal and professional life will be greatly enriched and enhanced as you discover and implement listening techniques fit for a leader.

What You Need to Know About Listening

Here's something a bit disturbing. Did you know that in a typical day we spend 75 percent of our time communicating and that 53 percent of *that* time is spent listening?[2]

We only have to look at the wasted productivity at work due to misunderstanding a message to underscore that poor listening habits are a negative ripple in our leadership pond. We only have to draw back the curtain on family relationships to see how hurt feelings, unresolved issues, and anger erupt when the message sent is not the message received.

Jesus' half brother James certainly understood the importance for leaders to develop effective listening skills. Soon after his opening remarks he makes the point that "everyone should be quick to listen, slow to speak and slow to become angry" (James 1:19). Who knows—perhaps James had witnessed firsthand the incident with the woman caught in adultery and learned from Jesus valuable listening skills.

The *Life Application Study Bible* expands on this idea: "When we talk too much and listen too little, what we communicate to others is that we think our ideas are much more important than theirs. James wisely advises us to reverse this process. Put a mental stopwatch on your conversations, and keep track of how much you talk and how much you listen. When people talk with you, do they feel that their viewpoints and ideas have value?"³

Note that there is a difference between hearing and listening. Our ears may physically pick up on sound waves and tones—therefore we hear. This may be why Jesus, in Matthew 11:15, said, "He who has ears, let him hear." What He was saying is that if you can hear these words, try to *understand them.*

Listening takes place when there is an understanding of the message conveyed, more than just an acknowledgment of the message. Do we look at the situation through the eyes, past experience, and feelings of the person conveying the message? If so, we can experience great empathy and *feel* the message as well as hear it.

You've probably seen several of the popular communication models available from research studies. Basically, the diagram illustrates the sender, the message, the channel such as a speech, the written word or music, and the receiver.

sender ———— message through a channel ———— receiver

Sounds so simple, doesn't it? But add to the message emotion, voice inflection, loaded words, body language, and the predisposed attitudinal state of the receiver and, well, we can really have a huge misunderstanding on our hands.

In fact, more likely than not, as the sender is giving her message, the receiver is already anticipating what the message will be and creating her own response to what she thinks the message is. She may never correctly understand the intended message because she never really heard it or listened to it. This is the person who finishes all of your sentences for you—sometimes accurately, but most times not.

This must explain why the disciples, who had heard Jesus explain many times about His death and resurrection, acted like total idiots when things started to unravel after Judas' betrayal. They reacted as if they had never heard—or should I say, understood—a thing Jesus had predicted. Obviously they interpreted everything Jesus had to say about a heavenly kingdom as pertaining to an earthly kingdom—their own preconceived notion. Why else would James and John (and their mother too, mind you) earlier have requested that they sit on the right and left of Christ when He came into His kingdom? (Mark 10:35-45) And this, just following another of Jesus' clear predictions about His death. They obviously had adopted a predisposed idea that Jesus would come to power on earth as their Jewish King during their lifetime. This assumption made it impossible for them to understand the correct message Jesus gave time after time.

Here is another interesting fact about the listening process: There is a differentiation between the number of words we speak and the number of words we can hear with comprehension. The average speaker's rate is between 100 and 150 words per minute, whereas a listener can comprehend up to 500 words per minute. Consequently, over three quarters of our listening time is "spare" time.[4] What fills up the time difference? Well, this is where the problem lies and the possibilities are endless. We daydream, notice movement behind the speaker and are distracted; we anticipate the message and prepare our response; we totally tune out the speaker's words and don't even hear them. These are bad listening habits worthy of breaking.

Other negative habits that keep us from correctly understanding a message include calling the subject boring, criticizing the speaker's ability, getting overstimulated, listening only for fact, faking attention, trying to outline everything, avoiding hard-to-understand material, and letting emotionally laden words bother us.[5] With all that going on in our heads, no wonder it's difficult for us to comprehend and remember many messages.

Definition of Listening

Just to clarify exactly what is meant when we talk about the listening process, let me list several ideas to get us started. (We will add to these ideas as we go along.) Notice that listening is a proactive, not passive, experience:

Listening is:

- An interactive process

- Involves understanding

- Requires participation—acting upon an idea

- Forces us to match meanings

Listening is not:

- Talking

Listening requires:

- Screening out distractions

There are typically five ways we respond while listening:

- Evaluation, or judging what has been said

- Advice, or attempting to solve the speaker's problem

- Preoccupation, or giving no gesture of communication

- Question, or attempting to gain more information

- Paraphrase, or attempting to communicate back the speaker's content and emotion

During routine classroom exercises involving the listening process that I've conducted over the years, scores reveal that most people listen at a 50 percent efficiency rate. This means that right after hearing a speech or being involved in a conversation, most people experience a take-away value (what they understood and remembered) of one half. Can you guess what the take-away value is after forty-eight hours? It's less than 25 percent!

Some of this is due to the way our memory functions. Our short-term memory area in the brain can hold only five to six items for about five seconds.[6] Our long-term memory, however, retains information that can be retrieved many years later. As listeners, we must find ways to store important items in long-term memory. This takes concentration but can be done through repetition and association. It also requires the development of effective listening skills.

What Happens When We Don't Listen?

Obviously, poor listening skills have adverse consequences. Effective leaders at home and in the workplace recognize the importance of developing good listening habits as a way to prevent problems. Here are some possible consequences of poor listening habits:

Misunderstandings Abound

Not only do we get either part or all of the message wrong when we don't listen, but we are apt to repeat that incorrect message to someone else. That person, using the same bad listening habits, changes our meaning and passes it along to someone else. We used to play a little game of telephone tag as an icebreaker at parties where one person whispered a brief story into the ear of the person next to her. Then that person whispered to the next person and on and on around the circle. The last person, of course, was asked to say out loud the message that she received. Any chance that her message was the same as the one given at the beginning? Not one!

While telephone tag is a fun exercise at a party, the consequences of misunderstandings on the job or at home can be emotionally devastating and expensive.

People Feel Hurt

Every person yearns to be valued and appreciated. She feels this way when she knows that her ideas have been correctly interpreted and understood. This doesn't mean that we agree with every opinion that is expressed to us, but if we want to see contentment and productivity, we need to avoid hurting those willing to communicate with us. We hurt others when we brush off their ideas and don't take time to hear them out. And how is a person with a wounded spirit most likely to act after being treated this way? Her ideas will stay within the confines of her dreams and we may miss out on some great ideas and innovations because of it. She will feel less valued and less valuable. What a loss to her and to the group. Her contributions will never be enjoyed.

People Are Less Motivated

When we allow others to offer solutions and give them opportunity to provide direction, they take ownership, which leads to productivity. Consider the worker who sees how the assembly line can be more efficient, but when he expresses his idea to his manager, gets nowhere. How often will this person continue to look for and express creative solutions? Most probably he will shrug and decide to just keep working the job the same old way, which may take longer and cost more in the long run.

Mistakes Are Made that Lead to Unplanned Expenses

My husband recently experienced this frustration. He had given instructions for a letter to be sent out that needed to include several sections of valuable information. In the busyness of the day, an important list of people endorsing their cause was left out of the letter. Luckily for him, he caught the mistake and the letter was corrected. Unfortunately, it was *after* the letter had been printed and was ready to mail. The corrected version had to be printed again. His staff and printing expenses were doubled because the message given was not the message received.

What Happens When We Do Listen?

Fewer Mistakes Are Made

Active listening involves repeating, clarifying, and asking questions. If something is not clear, the effective listener must take the responsibility to make sure her understanding is accurate. This will avoid costly and time-consuming mistakes.

I remember an occasion when double checking averted disaster. I was invited to give a concert at a church that I had never been to before. Just before I headed out the door I called to clarify the directions, and it was a good thing I did. The directions I had written down were incorrect. Had I not decided to clarify that the directions were as I had understood them, I probably would have gotten so lost that I would have missed the event. All those people who had depended upon me to provide special music at their service would have been disappointed.

People Feel Affirmed and Understood

When we make all attempts to understand what we are being told, we bring value to a relationship. When people feel valued, they feel that someone understands them and their ideas, and therefore are affirmed and encouraged to continue expressing ideas and solutions. Affirmed people are satisfied workers and self-confident family members. Isn't it interesting that peace and contentment can be experienced simply because we feel understood?

We Learn New Things

If you are doing all the talking, you will only be repeating information you already know. How much more beneficial for you and me to sit back and listen as new information is being provided by those we are in conversation with. The things we learn by listening could be critical pieces of a puzzle we have been trying to solve.

Collecting Data Through Effective Listening Solves Problems

Herman Miller is a world-renowned furniture manufacturer whose success in great part is based upon listening. When faced with a line problem or sales issue, those in leadership look for answers among their coworkers. It's not unusual to see a group of people crawling around a machine or furniture model exchanging ideas and sifting through the data to solve a problem. No matter the title or position, each person is allowed an equal-valued opinion during the listening exchange. Questions are asked that clarify; the information offered is offered back in different words—paraphrasing; and evaluation of the idea is withheld until all data has been collected. More times than not, the problem is solved and each individual takes ownership in providing a solution.[7]

How Can We Be Better Listeners?

By looking at the pitfalls of poor listening and the advantages of effective listening, it's clear that leaders are most productive if they can be better listeners. Here are several things to keep in mind as we brush up on and practice our listening skills:

Truly Care About Someone Else

I asked Florence Littauer, author and humorist who *loves* to talk and tell wonderful stories, her advice on being a better listener: "I've been around people who have taken listening classes and they *do* all the right things— lean in, nod, and say 'uh huh,'—but deep down inside they don't really *care* about the person who is speaking. We must really care for others before we can master the art of listening."

Mary Kay Ash, founder of Mary Kay Cosmetics, imagines that every person she meets is wearing a sign around her neck that says, "Make me feel important!"[8] And how can we do this? By simply asking "how do you feel about that?" or "tell me more."

Try to See the World Through the Other Person's Experience

It has been said that everyone sees the "map of the world" from a different place on the map. The world looks very different if you're in the valley, compared to when you're on the mountaintop. Therefore, as effective listeners, we need to see the world from the other person's position on the map to understand her viewpoint.

A woman once demanded that we refund her registration fee for one of our TimeOut for Women! conferences. We do not typically do this, but I usually try to find out what's behind the request before restating our policy. Our first phone call to her revealed that she felt the conference was too emotional. I reflected on the conference from my place on the map and admitted that there were a couple of tearful moments, but nothing that I considered overly emotional.

Probing a little more using statements like "tell us more," and "so you feel that . . ." allowed the woman to get to the heart of the matter. She was disturbed by a very poignant true story one of our speakers had told about a friend who died of breast cancer. The woman then revealed that her husband had just been diagnosed with cancer. No wonder this story hit her like a ton of bricks! Once we understood the emotions, fears, and life experiences she brought into the arena with her, we were able to understand better the things she saw from her vantage point on the map.

Take 51 Percent of the Responsibility

I taught high school for the better part of fifteen years, and you can imagine what kinds of attitudes I was greeted with each day. Typically the body language through crossed arms and slouching in the desk indicated the nonverbal message, "I dare you to teach me anything!"

In fact, during my second day of teaching my first year, two boys sat in the front of the classroom gazing at the blackboard that contained a quote for the day and a vocabulary word. Appropriately, this day's word was "apathy." They both stared at the word, mildly interested, when one tried to pronounce the word: "a-PATH-ie," "Apthly," then finally, "What *is* that word?" The other shrugged and sighed, "Do you think I really care?"

Obviously these teens were going to put as little effort as possible into the exchange of communication between us, leaving the responsibility for them to understand the message up to me. Effective listeners don't make the idea exchange the job of the speaker, but take the bulk of the responsibility. Three important ways that a listener takes responsibility include paraphrasing, empathizing, and clarifying.

Paraphrasing takes place when the listener rephrases the meaning of the message sent so that the speaker can judge whether the message intended was the message received. Good paraphrasing phrases include, "in other words . . ." or "so what you're saying is . . ."

Empathizing goes deeper than understanding the message, but captures the emotion of the message. Empathy is really the opposite of apathy: "A mental entrance into the feeling or spirit of another person or thing."[9] So you feel that . . ."

Clarifying involves asking questions and making restatements which make the message very clear. "So how did that work again?" "If I understand it, you say that . . ."

These three techniques allow for the pace of the conversation to slow some, which gives us ample opportunity to think through and question the message we think we are receiving.

Don't Prepare Your Next Statement

How often are we guilty of pondering the next brilliant point we're planning to make while we are supposed to be listening? While it's true that there is a constant exchange of sending and receiving in a conversation, effective listeners work toward focusing on the speaker and her words rather than preparing the next statement.

Wait to Hear the Entire Message Before Responding

If you're like me, I love to finish sentences for people *and* interrupt them with my new and better idea! Good listeners make an effort to hear the entire message before responding. Patiently waiting also helps us not to jump to quick conclusions, which could very well be incorrect.

Implement the "Golden Pause"

When we get to the "Duh" chapter on improving speaking skills, you will find the Golden Pause is the most effective speaking tool a speaker can employ. It is also the most valuable listening skill.

Here's how it works: The Golden Pause is a three- to four-second silence used in two distinct places in conversation:

- After you respond to a message

- After the sender transmits the next message

The Golden Pause draws out information such as facts and emotion from another person. It is a technique many reporters use. Many interviewees cannot stand the silence as the cameras roll so they rush on to fill up the silence with comments—sometimes giving out more information than they had intended.

Learn to Hear Body Language

You've probably heard the familiar phrase, "Your actions are so loud I can't hear what you're saying." Much effective listening takes place when we notice what is *not* being said. Here are some things to take note of so that you likely will receive the correct message.

Eye contact

Think of the things that our eyes reveal about us. A doctor can look into our them and tell many things about our physical condition. It is said that Oriental jade dealers used to wear sunglasses while negotiating because when they spotted a particularly valuable gem, their pupils dilated, thus giving away their excitement.[10]

Watching the eyes can reveal truthfulness, or lack of it, and emotions such as joy or sadness, shame, embarrassment, disagreement, and dislike. Eyes can also reveal low self-esteem or shyness. The tuned-in listener can gather information beyond the spoken word when looking deeply into the eyes of the speaker.

Facial Expressions

My husband maintains that my face is an open book to my soul. No matter how I try, if I'm angry, hurt, irritated, impatient, or tickled, I wear it on my face. In fact, I tend to blush when embarrassed, and I've never found any way to mask this obvious outer expression of inner feeling.

An effective listener makes note of any grimace, change, or tightening in facial muscles, a smile, or even a frown. She also evaluates whether the facial expression is the same message given by the eyes. Sometimes a person can mask emotions in every facial feature—except the eyes.

Breathing Patterns

The speaker's breathing patterns can often give clues to deeper messages. Slow, shallow breathing would indicate a relaxed, honest communicator. Rapid breathing could mean excitement—either from fright or from something positively joyful. Noting a shift in breathing during a conversation may indicate a change in attitude.

Posture

We can determine much by a person's posture. If she leans forward to speak with enthusiasm, we know that there is a rapport and connectedness forming. If, however, the speaker has hunched shoulders, or her head is down, we may get the impression that she is avoiding us or is feeling depressed. Leaning back or shifting the body away from us may indicate a sense of disassociation.

Gestures

Body movements that accompany the spoken word are often used to help illustrate a point. Common gestures include "drawing" pictures with our hands, using hand or head movement to stress words and stories, or actually pointing in the direction of the place or thing being discussed. Gestures can also include other telltale signs of the speaker's inner thoughts and motivations. When I'm conversing with someone who is chewing gum wildly while her foot is wriggling back and forth, I get the sense that she is impatient and preoccupied, don't you?

Vocal signals

Other signs that help us correctly translate the speaker's words include volume, vocal tones, and rate of speech. When our child rushes in from the school bus after school to relay a particularly exciting story about the tornado drill, her voice will probably be sky-high, loud, and fast. Not only do her words relay to us her message, but so too does the way she delivers them.

It would certainly not be fair to give heavy emphasis to a person's nonverbal message entirely by these signs, because there are no absolutes. Slouched posture may only mean that she has a headache or is tired. However, if we are attentive to the possible secondary messages sent through the nonverbal, we will certainly be more effective listeners.

How Can Better Listening Techniques Help Us to Be Better Leaders?

We Can Diffuse a Potentially Damaging Situation

We've all experienced it at some time or another—an emotionally distraught coworker or family member whose anger erupts to the boiling point. The person becomes animated with large gestures, loud voices, and heated body language. Whether the anger is directed toward us or someone else, there are two ways that we can initiate diffusing the situation.

Mirroring: when we look into a mirror, our reflection mimics each movement we make. It's typical of our human nature to mirror or mimic someone else's image as well. Therefore, if our son gets thrown out at home plate when he was clearly safe, we can either stomp right behind him into the dugout screaming at the ump or set forth calm gestures, vocal tones, and nonverbal messages for our son—and the umpire—to mirror. I've seen many a student fistfight broken up this way by trained teachers and principals who set the example of correct behavior for the student to imitate. Gaining and maintaining eye contact with a distraught person keeps her focused and is also a diffuser.

Paraphrasing: don't mistake paraphrasing as a statement of agreement. Paraphrasing is restating another person's ideas in your own words to show you understand. I once participated in a group exercise that called for us to work with a partner. The assignment was to purposefully give our opinion on a heated issue with which the other person disagreed. My partner supported abortion rights. I do not. That seemed like a very volatile issue for us to discuss.

Amazingly, it wasn't a conversation involving conflict at all. I stated my position and he repeated back my stance using phrases like "So you feel that

. . . I understand you to say . . . So what you really mean is . . ." I, in turn, repeated his ideas in the same way. Both of us felt that the other's ideas had been heard, understood, and that the message had been interpreted correctly without disagreement or open hostility. People have a greater need to feel understood than to be agreed with.

Listening Can Solve Our Problems

Years ago I heard Paul Harvey tell the story of a truck driver who paid no heed to the height sign on the underpass he was attempting to drive through. As a result, his tractor trailer became hopelessly wedged between the pavement and the bridge above.

Soon fireman, wrecking crews, and engineers were brought to the site to try to figure out the best way to free the trailer. As they were circling the vehicle, measuring, brooding over, and exchanging possible solutions, an eight-year-old boy kept tapping on shoulders, clearing his throat, and saying, "Excuse me." Yet no one paid him the least amount of attention.

Finally, the boy did get the attention of one of the engineers who stooped down to listen to what the boy had to say. He whispered, "Why not let the air out of the tires?" Well, now. How 'bout that? From the mouth of babes!

Listening to Godly Counsel Helps Us Make Good Decisions

Just consider the diverse personalities and professional experiences represented by each chosen disciple. Matthew was a tax collector, so we assume that he was the CFO. John the Beloved must have had a heart as big as all outdoors, so perhaps he was the VP for public relations. Peter, whose outspokenness sometimes got him in trouble, nonetheless was a risk taker for Christ and certainly acted as a successful advertising agent for the ministry. Thomas, perhaps unfairly coined as the doubter, may have been the critical listener who asked the tough questions before launching into Peter's hasty plans. What an interesting group dynamic Jesus created with each person He asked to follow Him.

Once Christ was resurrected and had ascended, the Acts disciples made calculated decisions based upon prayer, their past experience with Christ, and counsel with the Christian leadership of their day. We can assume that through watching and experiencing the leadership of Jesus for three years they patterned their own mode of business after His ministry. They knew where to seek out godly counsel and effectively listen to the guidance given.

Proverbs 15:22 reminds us that "plans fail for lack of counsel, but with many advisors they succeed." Seeking and listening to godly counsel is one of the best leadership qualities we can embrace.

Listen to Those Who Work Closest to the Problem

I once heard what I presume to be a true story that demonstrates this point. One of the major airlines was trying to figure out ways to cut back on meal expenses. The executives were smart enough to ask the flight attendants for feedback, since they work closest to the customer. One attendant noted that most of the trays she picked up after the meal was served still had the olive on it, which meant that it was not a high-demand food item for the customer. The airline decided to eliminate the olive and ended up saving over $40,000 per year.

When we listen to the nurse who knows her patient well, the janitor who knows which cleaning solutions work best, the teacher who understands which training materials are most effective, it helps "define our reality." All this means is that when we understand the truth and get correct information, we will provide clear direction for others. Some of our information may need to be filtered, but when we define reality through listening to those who work closest with those we want to serve, we can more effectively meet their needs.[11]

Listen by Watching What People Do

I attended a leadership conference in Chicago where a senior executive with Apple Computer, Guy Kawasaki, gave a keynote address. He illustrated the value of listening to what people *do*: Sony put together a teen research group to explore the trends in electronic devices. The payment for participating in the group was that each teen would be given a sample of the electronic prototype.

The teens discussed with the engineers all of the gadgets they thought would be cool on a boom box—the large, portable combination radio, cassette player, compact disc unit. When asked what color they thought would sell best to their age group, they unanimously decided yellow.

So, the engineers got to work and created samples of this new design. Wisely, they made samples in yellow and in black. The teens were then reassembled and introduced to the prototype they had helped design to test it and make additional comments. At the end of the session they were graciously thanked and told that each of them could choose a boom box to take with them.

Each one of them picked up a black one and left. That year, Sony produced this model not in yellow, but only in black.

Listening requires that we be sensitive to not only what we hear, but also to what we don't hear. Actions often will speak louder than words.

The Cure for Anemic Listening Skills

If we're honest, we must admit that most of our listening skills are a little anemic and could stand a prescription that will reverse our sickly symptoms! Using the acronym CURE, here is an easy way for us to remember the essentials of being a better listener—which ultimately will make us better leaders:

Comprehend the message through

- Sensing

- Interpreting

Understand the meaning by

- Filtering out distractions

- Looking at it from the viewpoint of speaker

- Being conscious of emotions

Respond by

- Asking questions

- Clarifying

- Paraphrasing

Evaluate to determine a proper response

Listening to Truth

We hear thousands of voices and messages each day, including the static from distractions that confuse and distort the messages. How do we successfully filter out the important and leave the waste behind? Just as harvesters used to collect wheat into round shallow dishes to be thrown in the air to separate the chaff from the wheat, we must somehow filter out the useless and often harmful information so that only the seeds of truth remain.

Matthew 17:5 finds Jesus on a high mountain visiting with Moses and Elijah while Peter, James, and John stand off watching in amazement. Jesus becomes transfigured into a brightness unlike any earthly equal. Then, can you even imagine this? The very voice of God booms from heaven His love, pride, and affirmation of His Son: "This is my Son, whom I love; with him I am well pleased. Listen to him!"

This is the only way that we can successfully evaluate and determine the proper response to the messages that have been conveyed to us. If we *first* listen to what Jesus has to say about it, He becomes the rudder of our ship, guiding us to safety, helping us to successfully plot our course.

Yes, Jesus still speaks to us today through what we hear: look to nature, acknowledge those creative thoughts that come from "nowhere" as His, trust the discernment of judgment He so faithfully provides, and most of all—listen to the written Word, since these words were first spoken words, intended for us to "listen to Him."

John 1:1 calls Jesus the Word. Think of it—a spoken word from the Almighty commanded the heavens and earth to be formed. Even the void heard and understood His voice. Then, the very breath breathed by the Word caused Adam to become a living soul. Hebrews 4:12 tells us that the Word is more powerful than a two-edged sword. "For the word of God is living and active. Sharper than any double-edged sword, it penetrates even to dividing soul and spirit, joints and marrow; it judges the thoughts and attitudes of the heart." Whether spoken or written, God's Word represents and reveals truth.

So powerful is God's written Word that it has endured millenniums, wars, famines, riches, greed, and evil men who have tried to quench it and destroy it. The written Word is a permanent record of words and deeds for generations to treasure and learn from. An ancient saying goes: "Short pencil better than long memory."

In 2 Corinthians 3:3, Paul tells us that we ourselves are a letter from Christ to the world. "You show that you are a letter from Christ, the result of our ministry, written not with ink but with the Spirit of the living God, not on tablets of stone but on tablets of human hearts." Wow! What does the world read and hear when it watches us living out Christ's letter?

Heavenly Father, we long to hear Your words of truth. Help us to clearly understand the messages You send to us so that we can, in turn, be a love letter from You to a world that needs You. Amen.

Uh . . . That Is, What I Really Mean to Say Is . . . Uh . . .
The Six Rs of Right Writing

Putting pen to paper lights more fires than matches ever will.
Malcolm Forbes[1]

So what is a chapter about writing doing in a book on leadership development anyway? What does writing well have to do with leading well? Plenty.

Consider with me for a moment the letter, diary, and history writers of the Bible. Would you agree that taking the time to permanently record miraculous events, the words and works of Jesus, and notes of encouragement to new believers has value? To me, the Bible is the most miraculous work of writing ever penned, especially when you consider the number of writers who spanned thousands of years, lived in different areas, and spoke different languages; yet, each word reflects the continuity of truth and from beginning to end points to a loving God.

We could learn much from these writers and their writing techniques, but for a moment, let's just consider their motivation—beyond God's inspiration. Here are a few things that propelled them into prolific proficiency:

- They wanted to provide a permanent record of events so there would be no diversion from the truth in the retelling.

- They were passionate about God.

- Their hearts were tender toward the lost, broken, and needy.

- They used the written word as an encouragement to others who lived far away or who were discouraged.

- They were out to make positive changes in the world.

These heart-directed motivations are the same sparks that ignite a woman today to make a positive impact in her sphere of influence. And, often, she must use writing as her avenue to convey information, make needs known, and instigate positive changes.

Before embarking on our own writing journey, let's take a brief side trip to Rome, Corinth, Galatia, Ephesus, Philippi, Colosse, and Thessalonica from 51 A.D. to about 57 A.D. You've probably guessed that letters to Christians in these cities were eloquently written and organized by the Apostle Paul.

Take a moment to review the first few paragraphs of each of these letters and you will discover several excellent writing techniques that will work well for us too:

The Opening

Paul uses the same greeting or salutation in each letter: "Grace and peace to you." In some of the letters he gets a little more verbose and adds "from God our Father and Jesus Christ."

Do you have a standard greeting that sets the stage and prepares the heart of the recipient? If not, have you thought of developing one? How would you like your reader to feel after reading your first words?

The Introduction

Paul immediately either gives thanks or positive praise. The only exception to this is while writing to the Galatians, since this was a type of reprimand document. Still, his greeting is full of positive truths, which gives the reader encouragement, and a good feeling so that he or she will read on.

The Body

Paul gets to the point right away. He doesn't waste the reader's energy or time by giving unnecessary information. Also, he clearly organizes his thoughts so that each point can stand on its own merit.

The Style

Paul is aware that there will be multiple readers of his work, both Jew and Gentile, male and female, educated and noneducated. He makes sure that his writing has broad-based appeal.

Restating the Purpose

Paul makes clear his "to do" statements at the beginning and end of his letters.

When you read through these books, you will see how Paul presented his information to convey how belief systems, behavior, feelings, and actions would glorify God. When you have done that, come back to this section and you will see how the Six Rs of Right Writing are based upon Paul's classic and timeless model.

So, in much the same way as Paul, you want to be an advocate of positive change. Let's take a look at how you can use these tools in everyday life. Many of us, at one time or another, have been members of the Parent Teacher Association, or the PTA. Let's say the PTA has asked you to create a proposal to send to the school board assessing the safety of playground equipment. While your work may not require the deep spiritual overtones of Paul's writing, if you model your work on Paul's, the strategy for writing will be much the same.

You sit down ready to begin and suddenly your mind is as blank as the sheet of paper in front of you. Well, maybe it will be easier at the computer. So you fire it up, place your fingers on the home keys, and realize that the cursor on the blank screen is lulling you into a hypnotic trance. Don't panic. Everyone needs a spark to help ignite the creative fuel in the mind.

Have you done your homework? Do you know enough about your topic to write about it intelligently? Are there places you should go to study the issue first? People to talk to?

Keep in mind that writing is probably one of the most difficult of the communication genres. As writer Olin Miller once quipped: "Writing is the hardest way to earn a living, with the possible exception of wrestling alligators."[2]

Okay, so you might not be a professional writer. You don't need to be. There are issues that we will feel compelled to wrestle with, and our most formidable weapon is the pen.

American humorist and novelist Mark Twain reminds us that "A powerful agent is the right word. Whenever we come upon one of those intensely right words in a book or newspaper the resulting effect is physical as well as spiritual, and electrically prompt."[3]

How, then, can we ally ourselves to the "right words" so that we aren't just staring at that blank sheet of paper or being mesmerized by that annoying cursor?

In this chapter we're going to discover six basic guidelines that will provide a simple structure and easy checklist to refer to each time you decide to wrestle with an issue through the medium of the written word. These ideas will serve you well for letters, memos, and business proposals. So, ladies, on your marks and sharpen your pencils, because we're going to ignite some fires with our written words.

The First R of Right Writing: The Receiver(s)

Whether we're talking advertising, marketing, or writing a note, our first consideration must be *who*. That is, to whom are we targeting our message? So before even tapping out that first paragraph, take a few moments to analyze your audience. Keep in mind that not only should the document be designed for the person you've addressed it to (Primary Reader), but that there will also be others, like a secretary, colleague, or mail clerk, who may read your message (Secondary Readers). I've often wondered if the Apostle Paul ever realized when he was writing to specific people of his time that two thousand years later, millions of us would be secondary readers of his manuscripts and gaining just as much from them.

Note that in our culture, sometimes it's more important to get our message past the secondary reader. I can't tell you the number of times a women's ministry director will confess to me that her pastor or secretary threw away information about a women's event because he or she didn't think she would be interested in seeing it. We once toyed with the idea of having a statement printed right on the outside of our TimeOut for Women! envelope stating: "GIVE THIS TO YOUR WOMEN'S MINISTRY DIREC-TOR! DO NOT THROW AWAY!"

Mass mailings certainly present a challenge in profiling the typical recipient. However, if you are targeting a specific person, you can successfully analyze the Receiver before writing anything. Pretend that this person is going to be your dinner guest and take time to become acquainted before the dinner party on several levels:

Primary Reader:

- Who is the primary reader?

- What is his or her decision-making style?

- Is this person a bottom-line person (needing only the facts), or does he or she require a logical rationale that leads to the bottom-line conclusion?

- Is your primary reader a people person, focused more on the who and the how?

- Is your primary reader a fact person, focused more on the what?

Secondary Reader

- Who are your secondary readers? (Who will open the document or receive a copy?)

- Do they have more influence than your primary reader? If so, how will that change the way you write your document?

- What views do the secondary readers hold that may influence the interpretation of your message, or how it will be acted upon?

- Are the secondary readers supportive or nonsupportive of your ideas?

Any time we communicate an idea, it's advantageous to analyze the targeted audience. This information allows us to adjust the content, tone, and organization of our message so that it has its greatest appeal to the Receiver. It also puts a face with our message so that we respect the position, experience, expertise, and feelings of the person we are addressing our comments to.

That letter from you and the other parents represented by the PTA takes into account that each recipient places its greatest earthly treasures on that playground every day at recess. Because of this, the Receivers of your document, whether secretary, principal, teachers, administration, or school board, will likely consider helpful any information you offer that contributes to the safety of children. Once you understand your primary and secondary readers, their priorities, values, and hopes for the future, you can then go to the next step, which is to consider the Reader's Situation.

The Second R of Right Writing: The Reader's Situation

Your reader's situation may greatly affect his or her response to your document. By researching the Reader's Situation, you may change the extent of your message, the request, or even the timing of when it is sent to maximize your chance of success.

Let's say that as a parent involved with the PTA, your correct conclusion is that the playground equipment is not safe. Screws and bolts are rusted and coming loose from the older slides and monkey bars. A couple of sinkholes have appeared on the ball field that could cause a child to sprain or break an ankle or leg. Some of the fencing is bowed and separating, allowing for unwanted visitors, or for a child to stray from the playground. All of these are serious and valid points that need attention. You've done your homework and realize that it's likely that these repairs or replacement costs could exceed $20,000 or more. How will you state your message if the last millage was turned down, equipment cutbacks made, and teachers laid off? Would you take a different approach as to how the funding could be raised for these repairs if this were the scenario? When would you send your document?

The Reader's Situation could cause you to change the extent of your information shared and response requested. Since the fencing and sinkholes might seem the most important and least expensive of the repairs, you might decide to limit your request to these items.

Perhaps there is a budget meeting coming up at which items like this are going to be discussed. You may decide to include in your proposal all of the repairs that are needed and present this information in your document for the budget committee to consider so it can add it to next year's budget. Or you may need to hold the requests until you know that the document will get to the decision makers who can act upon your proposal.

Before writing your document, consider all of the elements of your Reader's Situation:

- Timing

- Priorities

- Pressures

- Resources

- Risks

- Commitments

- Personalities

- Procedure

This list ended with procedure because this is a very important dimension of the Reader's Situation. If we do our homework and discover what the accepted procedure is in getting our document read, we can save ourselves heartache and time. Perhaps there is a special application that needs to be filled out or a specific committee assigned to receive such requests. Knowing the correct procedure helps us be more efficient and effective.

A little private investigating on our part, which includes learning about our readers and their situations, can direct our steps on the right path to getting to the right readers in the right situation. You wouldn't ask for a raise where layoffs are being made and you wouldn't try to raise donations for the playground from a major donor who had just lost his father to cancer. Gathering information and being sensitive to the Reader's Situation makes us aware of proper procedure, appropriate timing, and extenuating circumstances.

Now we can begin writing our document so that the *Reason* for its creation is evident and clear to our readers.

The Third R of Right Writing: Reason

Probably like me, you've read some letters that indicate that the writer's stated purpose was to bore us into a nap. Finally, the writer gets around to articulating the Reason for writing, but possibly this message is buried in page three of a five-page document, or at the very end.

During an executive training session I conducted, an adult student told a true story that confirmed how most readers thoroughly read the first page of a document, skim the pages in between, and read the last page. This particular student's boss sent out a three-page memo to over one hundred employees in his privately owned company. In the middle of the second page he placed the statement: "If you are reading these words, come to my office and claim a $100 bonus."

Not one employee came to claim the prize! This confirmed to the business owner that he should send out only one-page documents and should make it clear to the reader the Reason for the memo early on in his document.

Now isn't that a relief to know that you need to create only one page to get your point across? And it's recommended that you state your Reason in the first sentence.

It's this simple: "The reason I'm writing to you today is . . ." Or: "The purpose of my memo is to . . ." Grab that pencil or find the home keys on your keyboard because now you can begin writing. Use this simple method every time you begin a business document and you will have the right words to start writing, plus you'll save your reader from having to play hide and seek in for your Reason for writing.

After you've written the first draft, you may want to go back to the beginning and state your Reason more creatively, but these key words are just the little shove you need to remove writer's block.

So how do you complete this first sentence? Consider what it is you want your reader to *do*. How do you want him, her, or them to respond? Typically, we want to influence one of four things:

- Action: What action do you want the reader to take after reading your document?

- Behavior: How do you want your reader to behave as a result of your message?

- Thought: How do you want your reader's mind to be changed by your message?

- Feeling: How do you want your reader to feel once you've relayed your information?

Once you've determined which of these responses you hope to influence, you can complete your Reason statement and you have your opener. If we continue with our letter to the school board, we can clearly state our Reason in our opener by saying: "The reason for this memo is to call your attention to dangerous and deteriorating playground equipment that will need to be repaired by next year." Obviously, the memo intends to call the board into Action and makes that very clear right from the beginning.

The Fourth R of Right Writing: Readability

"I have made this a rather long letter because I haven't had time to make it shorter."[4]

As bizarre as it seems, much more preparation, effort, and time is needed to create a concise, well-organized document than a longer one. Robin Horder-Koop, a vice president with the Amway Corporation, admits that her greatest challenge in writing is "getting to the bottom line." She says, "I have a tendency to want to give all the background first before getting to the point. I overcome this by writing out my points first, then organizing them in bullet points for others to read." Elisa Morgan, president of MOPS, says that she first writes down the Big Idea. This becomes her Reason for Writing statement and all other ideas flow from this one Big Idea.

Organization of a Message Is Fundamental to Its Success

The fundamental purpose of putting our ideas in writing is for the reader to logically follow our thought process and come to the same conclusion that we hold. The only way this can happen is if our message is constructed in such a way that it is clear, concise, and correct.

At the risk of sounding too much like the English teacher I am, I hope you will bear with me through these next very important steps. The success of your document depends upon how closely you follow this writing progression.

I've broken the elements of writing the body of your business document into six distinct categories. Once you have determined your primary and secondary readers, their situations, and written your Reason for Writing statement, you are ready to proceed.

Remember that this section is designed to make your document as easy as possible for the reader to understand so that later, he or she will understand your request and will respond appropriately.

Brainstorm (Cut Loose)

Here's the rule on brainstorming: there are no rules! Follow these fun instructions:

- Find a quiet place

- Have paper and pencil handy

- Think about all the things you could include in your message

- Randomly jot down any ideas that come to you

- Do not organize or categorize any of the thoughts, just write down any thought as it flows into your mind

- Do not debate the appropriateness or "rightness" of an idea

- Exhaust all of the possibilities

- Brainstorm individually or in a group. A group allows for an additional dimension and often makes the brainstorm ideas more diverse and effective.

Remember that there is no such thing as a bad idea. Some of the most harebrained ideas may have a golden thread in them that eventually weaves a beautiful tapestry throughout your written document.

Author and former English teacher Carol Kent suggests doing it this way: "Write down everything you already know about the topic you're working on. Then write down each resource you know of that will give you additional information (books, people, articles, organizations, etc.). You'll have way too much material, so you will have to outline the main points from this information, choosing the most powerful of the points as your *big* ideas."

Your brainstorm is not your message, but it is an avenue to discover which points to include in your message. In a one-page document, you may want to limit yourself to three main points. I often think of the main point outline as the skeleton of my document. Once those bones are in place, you need to develop a strategy before actually fleshing out your main points, which puts the muscle, organs, and skin on your document.

Strategy (Theme)

A strategy is nothing more than picking a theme for your document and organizing the main points in a logical order.

After you've outlined your main points, think through which idea ought to be mentioned first, second, third, and so on. If I'm writing longhand, I actually place a 1 in a circle next to my first point, a 2 in a circle near my second point, and so on. Sometimes I take a sheet of paper and rewrite point number one at the top, point number two at the top of a separate sheet, and so on so that I have lots of room to continue developing my strategy.

When you have done this, look back at your brainstorm and determine whether any of the points can be categorized under your main points. If so, list them there. Then, go back and determine which order these ideas should be mentioned under your main points.

This is sneaky, but you've just developed the outline for your document. Your first draft will now almost write itself. Author Judy Schruer suggests keeping this outline in front of you at all times. Then, as you begin writing, you know exactly which ideas to mention when. Your outline becomes the map that directs you from one point on your document map to the next until you've reached your final destination.

Style/Tone (Personality)

Okay, you've heard these dry terms mentioned in your high school or college writing classes and they are way too evasive. Try this instead: Personality. How can you best represent your personality so it can be heard and seen by the reader through your written words?

You can do this by choosing words and ideas that give your reader insight into the feelings within your heart. Here's a little trick to help you remember how to portray your style and tone through the acronym SWAP. Your document should create an atmosphere in which it is safe for ideas to be exchanged between your reader and you.

Sincerity: Write it the way you would say it, and speak from your heart.

Warmth: Write with a smile on your face and a good feeling about the recipient, and the document will take on warmth, which creates trust and friendship.

Affirmation: Keep in mind the admiration you hold for the recipient and the respect for his or her work, and he or she will feel affirmed by reading your words.

Professionalism: Even in a confrontational document, maintain professionalism by avoiding emotionally laden words, or accusations that hit below the belt.

Do your best to convey your openness to SWAP ideas, to listen and be heard. Your style and tone represents your personality, and the written document is a key you are placing in the reader's hand and heart in hopes that it will open up the door of communication for further conversations.

Content (Message)

Obviously, your document's main purpose is to effectively convey your message to your reader. You do this through the content, which is the substance (meat) of your concepts (ideas). Your content is the method you use to express your heart. You will want to pay special attention to Mechanics, Structure, and Reading Difficulty:

Mechanics include:

- Word choice: using the right words

- Grammar: using the words right

- Spelling: proofreading for what "spellcheck" misses

Keep in mind this poem that was circulated among employees at Coastal Corporation in Houston:

> *"I have a spelling checker.*
> *It came with my PC.*
> *It plainly marks four my revue*
> *Mistakes I cannot sea.*
> *I've run this poem threw it,*
> *I'm sure you're please to no.*
> *It's letter perfect in it's weigh,*
> *My checker tolled me sew."*[5]

- Sentence structure: use the simplest form of a word: (*use* rather than *usage*)

- Keep sentence length short: fifteen to twenty words per sentence

- Keep paragraph length to about six sentences

Layout (Appearance)

For a moment, shut your eyes and—mentally—sit in the chair of the person who will read your PTA document. Imagine the piles of papers waiting for his or her attention, the commotion in the outer office area, and the street noise outside the window. Empathize with the stress, responsibilities, and hectic schedule facing this person as your document smolders amid the desk clutter. You want your document to stand out from the rest of the desk mess with neon intensity that screams "read me first." Is this possible? I think so, if you present your message to help the reader receive the message quickly and easily. Here are some things to think about:

- Headings: Use a simple one-word or short phrase heading to introduce your main points. You can draw attention to the heading by using all caps or boldface print.

- White space: Too much copy is confusing and gives the impression that there is no structure or organization to a document. Make sure that your document provides plenty of white space in the borders and between the main points.

- Bullets: "Shoot" your ideas quickly to the reader by using bullets

  - They provide more white space

- They promote quick skimming for the main idea

- They give organizational structure to your document

- Boldface, italics, and underlining: Be careful not to overuse, or else they lose their effectiveness, but if you highlight the most important ideas and information the reader's eye will naturally be drawn to glance at these ideas first.

Another way to draw the eyes of your reader to your document is to make it look different and appealing. Recently, a young woman at our church was hired to teach in a school system where two hundred applicants had applied for the job. After the interviews were over, she asked how, out of all the applications, hers was chosen for consideration. She was hoping that her success in curriculum development, behavioral psychology, and life experience were the reasons. The superintendent shrugged and admitted, "Well, your résumé was on peach-colored paper and was easy to find on my desk."

Granted, she *was* the best person for the job, but the distinctive look of her résumé drew the initial attention to it.

Editing (Another Viewpoint)

Once you've developed your first draft, it's helpful to get another set of eyes to read your document for feedback. If you know someone who is excellent at grammar, punctuation, and mechanics, ask her to take a look at your work and improve it in any way.

If you have a confidant within your organization who understands the issues, ask her if all the important issues have been addressed in your document.

Sometimes, like leftover spaghetti sauce, writing needs to be shelved for a day or two and brought out later for consumption. A little aging or time/distance away from your writing will provide you with a fresh perspective before you edit your final draft and send it along its merry way.

A Continuous Circle

I love pie! My favorite is my mom's apricot pie that she makes for Christmas. There is another type of PIE that I often sample when I need to write. It has three pieces and their flavors are Plan, Implement (Write), and Edit. Writing is a continuous circle that requires us to repeat this circle until our document is baked and ready to remove from the writing oven.

After your first draft, revisit the planning stage, write some more, then edit again. Repeat, repeat, repeat until you know that your final draft is the best tasting PIE around!

The final two of the Six Rs of Right Writing are brief, but I saved them for last because I feel they are the most important.

The Fifth R of Right Writing: The Request (What to Do)

I once received a fund-raising letter that was two pages long and single spaced. It allowed for precious little white space, bullets, or headings. Although I felt that I skimmed it pretty well the first time, I completely missed what the organization was raising money for! I heaved a distressed sigh and suddenly wished that this chapter had been finished in time to fax it to the organization for its next letter!

This cannot be said too many times: Do what you can to help the reader get your point at first blush. *Make your request in your reason for writing statement!*

Let's go back to our playground equipment memo. The first sentence read: "The reason for this memo is to call your attention to dangerous and deteriorating playground equipment that will need to be repaired by next year."

School board members are busy people. They want the important facts right up front. If they choose to read further, through your use of headings for your main points and bulleting of the specific dangers, they can quickly get the gist of your message.

Repeat your request again at the end of your document. Not only should you repeat the request again, but you should list the specific ways you feel the problem can be solved. In this case, you would want to list the specific dangers of the present playground equipment, then itemize the cost of repairs and replacement.

You can highlight your request, which is the most important part of your document, by using boldface print, italics, or underlining. I don't suggest using all at the same time—it gets a little bit overdone.

You're almost done with this amazing document. There is one more important item you will want to include.

The Sixth R of Right Writing: The Response (Either/Or)

While you've done a great job of creating a clearly written, organized, and designed document, it could fizzle and vaporize into thin air in the hands of the reader if you fail to require a response.

I don't necessarily like threats, but sometimes putting an end date for responding and an "either/or" statement goes a long way to get action. And isn't our point of this to get action? Of course it is.

So, the final words in your document should include the expected response and the time you expect it: "I will look forward by May 30 to hearing your plans for repairing and replacing the dangerous playground equipment. If I do not get a response from you at that time, the PTA has asked that I inform the local newspaper of this safety issue."

Admittedly, this may be too strong, depending upon the extent of the problems. However, the point is that you have given a specific timetable and made it known that you expect a response to your document. I doubt that this memo will get put in a desk drawer or the trash.

What about E-mail?

Before closing this chapter, I want to share with you some pitfalls and solutions in writing e-mail documents, since letters, memos, and proposals have become so common in this electronic genre.

Pitfalls of E-mail:

- Poor grammar abounds

- Style and tone are often misconstrued

- Because it is immediate, the writer doesn't spend enough time editing and rewriting

- Too much information is given at one time, which confuses the reader

- The recipient receives many uninvited and unwanted messages

- It takes a great deal of time to read and respond

Advantages of E-mail

- It's quicker and cheaper than sending a letter

- It allows for a permanent, written record

- It connects us to organizations and people quickly and efficiently

- It allows us to quickly prioritize which messages we want to read first, if at all

- It's fun

Ways to Improve the Effectiveness of Your E-mails:

- Always place a subject in the subject line.

- Deal with only one topic per e-mail.

- Reread each e-mail you've written several times before sending to make sure that the tone is friendly and warm and the grammar is correct.

- Provide short, concise responses, but don't be too curt.

- When responding, either copy and paste the sender's document within your response and answer her questions as they were raised, or refer to what she asked you to respond to. I remember once not including anything in the subject line and receiving the response, "Sounds good to me. Go ahead." Go ahead and do what? I was totally lost!

- Take as much pride in using proper capitalization and punctuation and clear wording as you do in a nonelectronic document.

- Organize the layout of your e-mail the same way we've talked about in this chapter by using white space, headings, and bullets.

- Remember that your "old mail" file may run out of room quickly, so if you want to refer to an important document, save it and refile it on your hard drive or print out a hard copy. I've known authors to lose their entire book, college students their final exam research paper, and lawyers important agreements due to no backup.

- Confirm verbal conversations through a quick e-mail listing the main points that were discussed.

Another little trick my cowriter, Deb Mendenhall, and I use is to create each chapter in a word processing document, but rather than attaching it as a file and sending it, copying the text and pasting it right in the e-mail. The recipient can then copy and paste the electronic words into her own word processing program without losing any text! Deb has taught me *so* much about writing and with her help, I know that the expression of my ideas has been made easier for you to read.

Well, this turned into a Baker's dozen, didn't it? I hope that some of these ideas either confirm effective methods you already employ or give you some new things to think about. I must admit that I'm greatly relieved that e-mail has preceded widespread video conferencing through television simulcast. I hope I'm not the only one who e-mails early in the morning wearing my threadbare hooded robe and bright pink bunny slippers!

In summary, remember that your job as a writer is to help the recipient be a fast and efficient reader. Therefore, you must design your document so that it is easy to read, making sure that your request and expected response are included. If the document is brief, clearly worded, well-organized, plus laid out so that the reader can get the main idea in about three seconds, MISSION ACCOMPLISHED! You go, girl!

We've delved into two areas of communication and shown how listening and writing are valuable leadership tools. Now we're ready to hone your verbal skills so that you can polish your platform performance. Just as in writing, effective speaking spurs people into action so that the world can be a better place! Go get a glass of juice, walk around the block once (don't forget Fido), then let's move on to the next section.

Dear Father, I pray that the things You have written on the heart of my dear sister will overflow onto the pages of her writing. May each idea she expresses glorify You—the true Word. Amen.

five

Duh . . . That Is, Uh . . . Er . . . You Know . . . Well . . . Um . . . Anyway . . . Polishing Your Platform Performance

We once stayed in a five-star hotel where the front doors stretched over eight feet wide and—from top to bottom—were pure glass, etched with intricate designs like fine crystal. A six-inch band of radiant brass framed the glass. From time to time as we passed through the doors we noticed a hotel worker, polish cloth in hand, rubbing away the finger prints and street grime from the brass. He used a potent-smelling cleaner that, combined with the friction of the cloth and the persistent pressure behind it, kept the surface so bright that we could see our reflections.

Think of your skills as that brass frame. Each time you use them, or learn something new that will strengthen them, you are taking cloth in hand and polishing them so they will gleam a little brighter.

Polishing a skill, such as speaking, may also entail some friction, repetition, and persistence, much the same way that brass door stayed untarnished. If the skill is rusty or unpracticed, it will take a little more friction, repetition, and persistence to get it highly shined. However, maintaining a skill requires just a little buffing every now and then to keep its beauty and effectiveness bright and reflective.

Effective and influential leaders often must present their ideas before others; sometimes before a room full of others. If speaking in front of people is new to you, or if you've shied away from it for a long time, you may feel totally inadequate or rusty. If so, take some extra time with this chapter so that the helpful hints can penetrate, giving you encouragement as you learn how to lead and influence others through this powerful medium. If you are already a confident public speaker, don't skip over the chapter just yet. I think there will be some very new and different ideas here that will keep your presentation buffed up and ready to reflect God's truths.

I have taught public speaking to many executives who hold high profile leadership positions within their companies. Although they have influence through their titles and skills, they discover very quickly that if they don't have a way to express themselves articulately and confidently, they can lose their edge in being effective leaders. Whether making a point in a church meeting or persuading stockholders to invest, the game plan for articulating ideas is the same.

Image

What was your first mental picture when you read the word *image* above? A bright red sports car? A big diamond ring? A huge house in just the "right" neighborhood? These things might very well connote an image of success to those who measure success by expensive monetary objects. But, as a speaker, you will be hard pressed to drag along to each speaking engagement all of the material entrapments you feel could help you to project a successful image.

No, in this context, image refers to the impression someone has of *you*—for who you are and what you stand for—not what you have accumulated. The moment that we meet someone for the first time or get up to speak in front of a group of people, we project an image. Before we even begin the polishing of our speaking skills, it's important for us to consider what type of an image we project.

Consider this: most people form an opinion about a speaker within the first thirty seconds. That's not much time at all to create a positive image, is it? Yet within that first thirty seconds, or twenty-five words, the audience determines three things about the speaker:

Can they trust her?

Is her topic interesting and applicable?

Does her style and content provide value to them?

Now, I'm not trying to scare you, but the reality is that after your first thirty seconds in front of an audience, 25 percent of them will *not* like you. Another 25 percent will really like you, and the other 50 percent will take a wait-and-see attitude.

This is why a first impression is so important and why as presenters we must consciously work at providing an image that will be a lasting, positive impression. Image is *not* an act or an insincere role. It is a projection of our best intentions. Note this: *image is drawing attention to your best qualities and strengths.*

Do you know what your best qualities are? Do you know how to draw attention to them? In just thirty seconds, how can you present an image that will entice people to trust and listen to you?

Right now, take a few moments to list four of your most positive qualities. I'll get the list started and you can finish it:

1. I have a friendly smile.

2.

3.

4.

Let me challenge you to adopt an attitude that has helped many public speakers in creating a trustworthy image. It's very simple and it's also biblical: "Love your neighbor as your self" (Matt. 19:19).

As author and humorist Liz Curtis Higgs says, "Pray not that they [your audience] will love you, but that you will love them. You are not there to give a speech, you are there to change lives!" What better way to show our love to those we speak to than to keep focused on how our presentation might touch their hearts, be an encouragement to their weary souls, or inspire them to embrace a life direction that follows Christ.

Rapport

When we put the needs of our audience before our own, something incredible naturally erupts. It's called *rapport*. Rapport is a French word that literally means friendship. Rapport does several things:

- It creates "common ground"

- It radiates warmth

- It gains and keeps attention

- It develops a relationship

You can develop rapport by making direct eye contact, smiling, and using appropriate touch. However, the best way to develop a true friendship with an audience is to know it. In order to do this, we must correctly analyze who the audience is before we even meet it.

A friend of mine who is a conference speaker tells the story of arriving late for a speaking engagement years ago and being ushered into the auditorium during the opening prayer. She would be introduced immediately following the prayer. Until that moment, she really didn't know what kind of audience was present. So, during the short prayer, through one half-opened, squinted eye, she gazed around the room. It was suddenly apparent that this was an ultraconservative religious group that did not wear makeup or jewelry. She quickly removed her clip-on earrings and other jewelry so that she would not offend her audience. From then on, she implemented the important practice of analyzing her audiences before the event.

Analyzing Your Audience

You may be asked to speak to your church Bible study or make an announcement at a parent/teacher meeting. This is great, because you probably know personally many who will be present. However, if you are asked to speak to a group you do not know, here are five questions you *must* ask about them before you even begin preparing your message:

- What are their needs?

- What are their expectations of you?

- What are their hopes and values?

- What are their fears and concerns?

- How will they expect to see you dressed?

Can you see how the content, attitude, and motivation for your presentation all hinge on the answers to these important questions? Just think—if you don't understand their needs, how can you meet them? If you don't know what they expect of you, how can you provide them with content of value? If you don't understand their value system, how can you find common ground? If you don't understand their fears, how can you provide comfort?

I purposely included the last one about dress since our appearance is so important as we make that first impression. We don't want to wear athletic attire to a formal event anymore than we want to wear a business suit to an outdoor picnic. It's a good question to ask.

The Apostle Paul knew the value in assessing the makeup of his audience. Let's take a brief side trip to Antioch by way of Acts 13, where, on the Sabbath, Paul was standing to speak in the synagogue. Can you guess who his listeners were that day? He tells us: "Men of Israel and you Gentiles who worship God." He approached this particular audience with the Gospel by appealing to their common biblical heritage. His ideas and word choices reflect the rich history of Israel as was common to all of them there.

Contrast his analysis of that audience to that of another in Acts 17:22. Paul was in Athens, standing on the Areopagus, today known as Mars Hill. This is not a synagogue, but a marketplace with mixed nationalities and pagan religious attitudes. He was a master at finding that common ground so necessary in reaching an audience. He noticed their altar inscribed "To an Unknown God," and used the familiar to teach them about an unfamiliar. He knew of their pagan beliefs so could reconstruct the same message he had given in the synagogue to those here in the marketplace. Oh, that we are this astute in conveying our message with the same sensitivity to our audiences. I would guess that even the attire that Paul wore reflected what was accepted by each of these different cultures.

So, back to our century. Like Paul, you want to concentrate on drawing attention to your best qualities and strengths while keeping in mind the needs, expectations, values, and fears of your audience. But, just thinking about getting up in front of more than two people makes your hands sweat, your heart race, and your vision blur. What are you going to do to get yourself under control so that you can put even two words together that make any sense?

Presentation Anxiety

Isn't it nice that we don't have garbage men anymore? Now they're sanitation engineers. Gone are the days of the stewards and stewardesses; now they are flight attendants. There are few secretaries left either; we now have administrative assistants. Well, isn't it nice to know that we no longer suffer from stage fright? I bet you feel much less nervous now that you know that these days it's called presentation anxiety.

Oh, really?

I must admit that it feels the same to me too.

I once attended a large economic club luncheon where the keynote speaker walked to the podium, took off his glasses, and gazed leisurely around the hall. Apparently he had forgotten his notes and could not remember his opening line. Finally, after an awkward silence, he just smiled and shook his head. "You know," he managed to say, "the human mind is an amazing organ. It begins working the moment of birth and stops the minute we get up to speak to a group!"

Even this seasoned public speaker suffered a bout with presentation anxiety that day. Most people do. In *You and Your Network*, Fred Smith encourages us by saying, "Anxiety itself is not all important. What is important is what we do with the energy that anxiety creates."[1]

Miss Ellen Harvey is the dearest mentor I've ever had. From the first day I walked into her ninth-grade speech and drama class, she encouraged and challenged me to go the distance and climb the next step. On that first day of class in 1969, the quote of the day on the blackboard was "Enthusiasm is the X-ray of the soul." From 1978 on, when I began teaching my own high school speech classes, this has always been the first quote of the year on my blackboard as well.

I didn't understand this statement for a long time until Miss Harvey taught us how to channel our fears into positive energy that results in enthusiasm. I may *feel* nervous, but if I take the energy created by that fear and direct it properly, my audience will perceive my *image* as being enthusiastic and energetic. In fact, a little nervousness may just be the adrenaline I need to help me stay on my toes so that I keep my concentration. Presentation anxiety can actually be a *good* thing. If it were possible to X-ray my soul, would God see my fears turned over to Him so that they become enthusiasm? This is my prayer.

We attract what we radiate. If you don't believe this, purposely attach yourself to a very negative, bitter person and see if after a short time you don't begin to radiate negativism and bitterness too. In the same way, if we radiate joy, enthusiasm, energy, excitement, and peace, we will attract to ourselves these very characteristics—and draw them out of others as well. Zig Ziglar reminds us that Albert Einstein said we have to have seven positive influences to overcome one negative one.[2]

Think of the impact radiating enthusiasm can have on our audiences. If we get up there and smile, make eye contact, touch them with our compassion, and use a voice filled with expressiveness, what will likely be the feedback we receive? Yes! They will smile back at us, look us in the eye, and nod agreement. Just as we can use mirroring as an effective listening device, we must use mirroring as an effective speaking tool.

But, you say, I still have to cope with the outward signs of nervousness. True. In fact, there are probably five common nervous ailments you will suffer. However, they probably feel a lot worse than they look. Here are the five common signs of nervousness and a few tricks to help you cope with them.

Trembling/Shaking Knees

When we fear something, our body immediately responds with adrenaline so that we can flee and escape danger. This worked just great in cavemen times when a lion would sneak up behind us or we had to chase our dinner. However, when what we fear is getting up in front of people to speak, the adrenaline still does its job and makes us tremble.

Rather than bolting to a quick escape, we need to rid ourselves of the excess adrenaline. We can do this very simply by tensing and relaxing muscles.

When I was in high school I competed in a beauty—well, they called it a scholarship—pageant, but we all knew that we had exercised and dieted for more than showing off our brain power. When the big day finally arrived we were honored to host the current Miss America as our guest. We thought that she floated on air: "our ideal" as the song goes. She was there to grace the stage with her presence and sing a song for the audience during one of our costume changes. Since I was already dressed and just sitting on a crate backstage, I was excited to hear her sing.

To my utter amazement, during her introduction she began pacing frantically the whole width of the backstage area. Then, as if she actually held ten-pound weights in each hand, she began "curling." But then, it just got to be too much for me when she began inhaling through her nose and blowing out through her mouth. I thought she was going to explode. I was just about ready to ask her if she needed to breathe into a paper bag when her name was announced. She gracefully turned toward the stage, and as the spotlight caught her, she smiled and just floated out in her foam-green chiffon gown.

Granted, you and I don't always have the luxury of a hidden place to let off steam and rid ourselves of excess adrenaline; however, even while sitting in our seats waiting to be introduced, we can tighten and relax many muscle groups. If it's shaky knees, we should concentrate on tightening and relaxing the legs. If our arms or hands are trembling, perhaps we should pretend we are curling those ten-pound weights ourselves. Try this and see if it doesn't help ease some of your nervous trembling.

Shortness of Breath

We tremble because the adrenaline produced by our fear creates energy, making our heart beat faster. With a fast beating heart often comes shortness of breath. Miss America had the right idea on this one too. When we inhale through our nose and exhale through our mouth, we can often combat shortness of breath. It's also helpful to concentrate on slowing down the rhythm so that the breaths we take are longer and provide more oxygen to the body.

Sweaty Palms

Why is it that we seem to suffer sweaty hands only when we need to use them? The baseball player can rub his hands in the dirt to give a better grip on the ball, but a speaker or piano player seems somewhat helpless before an audience on this one.

Don't be embarrassed to bring a handkerchief to the podium with you. It may prove helpful in mopping your brow as well. Also, stand with your hands out to the side so that nature can dry them.

High-pitched Vocal Tones

Another very typical outward sign of inward nervousness is a higher pitched vocal range. It just seems like that ol' adrenaline does a number on our voices as well. If this happens to you, there are two things you can concentrate on: slow down your rate of speech and try to lower your vocal tone.

Even though some people are not musical, we all have different notes that we use when we speak. With thought and practice you can work on lowering your vocal tones so that you come across as confident and calm.

Dryness of Mouth

Perhaps it's because we are inhaling in and talking out of our mouth, but most presenters suffer a dry mouth. It is *so* important that the vocal cords be kept moist so that they can stay healthy. Drinking eight glasses of water per day doesn't only keep your body hydrated, but it also keeps your vocal cords strong.

One of my voice instructors once made a puzzling comment, saying that you know you are drinking enough water if you pee pale. I finally got it. The color of your urine indicates whether you are drinking enough water. The paler the color, the better for you.

In an emergency when water might not be available, you can just bite your tongue a bit to get a little extra moisture in your mouth.

Don't you feel better knowing that most presenters suffer a degree of nervousness and that these are the things they do to combat it?

Here's another interesting fact: *The Book of Lists* has, for many years, put public speaking at the top of the list of what people fear most. And my guess is that it will remain at the top for a long time to come. In closing I share some advice from women who have been wonderful role models and mentors to me throughout the years in the area of public speaking:

Millie Dienert, who led the prayer effort for the Billy Graham Crusades for decades, is a gifted speaker. Before she speaks she "asks the Lord to release her from herself so that she will be given freedom."

Public speech trainer and author Florence Littauer: "When I *know* my content and speak from the heart, it gives me confidence."

Author Carol Kent: "I try to arrive at least thirty minutes early and meet perhaps twenty-five to fifty people beforehand so that as I look out over the audience during my presentation, I see thirty to fifty pairs of friendly eyes!"

Elisa Morgan of MOPS, International: "I pray. A favorite is 'Cause me to be forgotten and You to be remembered. May I decrease while You increase' (from John 3:28-30)."

Madeline Manning Mims, Olympic gold and silver medalist: "I don't get nervous, I get *pumped*! I pray for the people I'm preparing to minister to and place my heart in a position to be sensitive to their needs via the Holy Spirit."

Singer and comedienne Kay DeKalb Smith: "I don't consider my audience as *x* number of people, but consider them as a bunch of *one*. In other words, they are each seeing me one at a time. That helps me to concentrate on the individual rather than the group."

Barbie Cooper, who pastors with her husband at Mount Paran Church of God in Atlanta, says: "I pray, 'Lord, I cannot do this without Your anointing. I have nothing to offer except Your Word. Put Your words in my mouth and grace me with the ability to communicate effectively for Your glory.'"

When Jesus sent out the Twelve, these were the instructions He gave to them: "Do not worry about what to say or how to say it. At that time you will be given what to say, for it will not be you speaking, but the Spirit of your Father speaking through you" (Matt. 10:19-20). When we too turn to the Father in prayer, He *will* give us the confidence to stand up for Him and will faithfully speak through us.

People Hear What People See

I alluded to these statistics in the listening chapter because what we hear through seeing is so important to conveying a total message. During the last twenty-five years these percentages have fluctuated by only a percentage point as new research is conducted.

Basically, the message we convey to people is perceived through body language, voice tone, and content. It is so shocking when we realize that 93 percent of our message is conveyed through body language and voice tone alone.[3]

- 56 percent of the information you share is relayed through body language

- 37 percent is conveyed through voice tone

- 7 percent is relayed through content

Now, this does NOT mean that you should put any less effort into your content. In fact, the stronger your content, the more effective your body language and voice tone will be. It's just interesting that it takes more than mere words to get an idea across.

Body Language

So, before you even walk onto that speaking platform, your audience is sizing you up. What kind of an image do you want to convey through your body stance, movement, and gestures? Let me make a few suggestions for you to concentrate on:

Posture: Although I never gained any height after fifth grade, I was for a while the tallest in my class. My mom and dad used to harp on me something terrible to display good posture. Finally, one of their comments stuck and has traveled with me throughout my life. Perhaps it may also help you concentrate on good posture: "Be proud of your height." Whether you never grew beyond my five-foot-two or you are over six feet tall, imagine that proverbial string being attached to the top of your head and someone pulling it straight up. It is God who has given us our stature. Why would we be ashamed of this gift and slump over as if we were refusing His gift?

Good posture connotes confidence, poise, and control. You may not even vaguely feel these things, but as you practice good posture, your image will be one of confidence, poise, and control.

Smiling: I've traveled all over the world and have been in countries where I was hard-pressed to find anyone who spoke English. Still, a smile is universally recognized and communicates the same thing in Chinese as it does in Greek, English, or Swahili. What happens when we smile? I'll bet that 99 percent of the time the person we smile at smiles back. It is said that it takes seventy-two muscles to frown and only fourteen to smile.[4] Hey, finally, a shortcut to exercise!

Smiling conveys confidence as well as trustworthiness. If we want our audience to have confidence in our message and to trust us, we can, through body language, begin that process before ever uttering a word.

Touching: I've heard it said that we need ten significant touches per day to feel significant. It's great that our American culture encourages a handshake greeting, rather than a bow or nod. This gives us permission to create an atmosphere of affirmation. Physical touching makes others feel good. If they feel good, they will be more receptive to our ideas and opinions. Remember how many people are lonely. Be the one to give them a significant touch or two.

Gestures: What do you do with your hands when you talk to a group? I've seen men stuff their hands in their pockets and jingle their change. I've watched the total demolition of a paper clip right before my very eyes. I even once witnessed a foam cup made into a single ringlet by the nervous fingernail of a presenter as he talked. (I was so fascinated that I didn't hear a word he said.) Other times I've wondered if the hands of the presenter were glued to the podium since they were never once used to express a point or add to it.

When used appropriately, gestures connote that the speaker is relaxed and at ease with her subject area and role as speaker. Hands should be kept above the waist and used logically to enhance a point. The size of the room determines the size of the gesture. For smaller groups in a smaller area, keep your movement confined to between your waist and shoulders. However, for large halls, don't be afraid to own your space. Use extended arms; walk the length of the stage. Allow your presence to be felt in every corner.

Attitude: Hey, I thought this discussion was about body language. Well, attitude affects body language. A joyful attitude puts a lilt in your step. Peace gives an aura of calm. Humor brings a twinkle to your eye. When you walk out there with a positive attitude, your inner enthusiasm is seen in your outward expressions.

Eye contact: I like what master communicator Liz Curtis Higgs says about eye contact: "The secret here is to look at *one* person at a time in your audience. Forget the old rule about scanning people's foreheads. Look into that person's eyes until you sense them connecting with you. It keeps you real in your delivery and lets your audience know, 'I'm speaking to *you!*' Believe me, each person you visually 'touch' will NEVER take her eyes off you after that personal bond is made!"

I would add that it is effective to pick out several people in different sections of an audience to make this intimate eye contact with. No matter how far back someone is sitting, make her feel that you are including her in your visual touch.

So, before even preparing the content of your presentation, prepare the presentation of yourself. Keep in mind what it is the audience will discern about you even before you open your mouth to speak. If in the first thirty seconds they can find you trustworthy, interesting, and authentic, you will have succeeded in establishing a rapport with them that will begin at the beginning of your presentation, and—hopefully—beyond.

Vocal Quality

Vocal quality accounts for 37 percent of our message effectiveness. After years of musical voice training and public speaking classes, the following are things I believe will help your vocal tones work for you.

Tone and pitch variety: Tone and pitch refer to the notes on the musical scale your voice speaks. Some or us have very low vocal tones, and others very high. The most effective speakers try to vary their tone and pitch to give interest and vitality to their presentations.

Think of Johnny One-note who was a monotone singer who sang only one note all the time. *How boring!* Our speaking voices also deserve the freedom to glide the musical scale. The next time you speak, record yourself and make sure that you are using the entire octave for your speaking pitches.

Articulation: Keep in mind the equation "enunciation + pronunciation = articulation." I've found two things that enhance articulation and "clip" words so they are easily understood. I've said to many a theater student: "Spit out your Ts and Ss." Try it some time. Make sure that you pay special attention to enunciating your words clearly by literally blowing out on these consonants.

Rate of speed: Inexperienced speakers allow the words to just tumble out as quickly as possible, as if there is a word derby going on and they have to use all the words up in a short amount of time. This is so unfair to the audience. People need time to assimilate and absorb an idea before being ready to understand another idea. If we mercilessly pound them with quick words, they feel as if one tidal wave after another has bombarded them. Slowing the rate of speaking allows them to come up for air.

Volume: My high school teacher Miss Harvey used to tell us to talk to the deaf lady in the back row. While it's true that the use of microphones has helped us greatly in projecting our volume, we still must make a special effort to reach that person in the farthest corner of our speaking area.

Projection: Closely related to volume, projection is actually a breathing issue. One word of caution here. If you are lounging all over the podium or leaning on it in any way, you have already ruined your chances of good posture and proper breathing. Try this exercise: Lie down on your back and place a book on your diaphragm. Breathe naturally. Notice that the book rises and falls as you inhale and exhale.

I recently discovered a voice coach who has a new slant on proper breathing for singers, in particular. Roger Beale, from Atlanta, Georgia, claims that the diaphragm is an agent for inhalation, but it is the abdomen muscles that are responsible for the exhalation. He maintains that we can get a better "chest" sound by breathing this way, rather than the old school. He says, "The abdominal muscles and the intercostal muscles (between the ribs) contract and do the work. These are your blower muscles. To exhale, just blow. It's that simple."[5]

Work toward breathing this way even when you are standing so that the strain of projecting air out of your mouth falls on the abdominal muscles, not on your vocal cords and throat. Proper projection will enhance your voice tones and give you more air with which to articulate your words. Proper breathing will also encourage good posture.

Delivery

Closely aligned with vocal quality is your delivery method. You can have great content but ruin its effectiveness by not rehearsing it enough to perfect its timing.

Liz Curtis Higgs emphasizes the importance of timing: "Deliver each point, story, example, humorous line—and then *wait*. Wait. Count beats if you have to. One—two—three. I simply *look* at the audience with a half smile. I might lift my eyebrows or roll my eyes or run a hand through my hair or *something* to let them know I'm waiting intentionally and let them in on the deliberateness of my actions. Especially with humor, this timing business is critical, but it matters with serious content too. People need time to *think* about what you have said and *process* it. They need time for the holy 'aha' to sink in."

As we discussed in the listening chapter, the use of the Golden Pause is probably *the* most effective speaking tool you can use in public speaking. At first, silence seems like a painful eternity as you stand wordless before an audience, but as you perfect the use of the *pause* and include it in your notes as a deliberate act, your timing will keep the attention of your audience and help them remember key points.

In addition, involve your audience in your presentation as much as possible. Do you have any idea what the most important word is in a person's vocabulary? Give up? It's her own *name*. Anytime that you can include in your presentation the names of people in the audience, you are allowing them to take ownership and participate in your presentation.

In fact, the most successful presenters are those who know how to get their audiences involved and feel as if they are in control of the presentation, not the presenter. And, isn't that the way it should be after all? Aren't we there to meet their needs and speak for their benefit? Too often presenters seem to have the attitude that they are superior and what they have to say is more important than what the audience wants to hear. It's ludicrous.

Moving about on stage and using facial expressions and gestures that will emphasize your words are other techniques that will enhance your delivery. Pretend these people are in your house and that you are there to host them. Since the stage *is* yours for the presentation, treat it as a familiar room in your own home.

Here's something that can hinder the effectiveness of your delivery: handouts. Do *not* pass out notes during the time you are speaking. Either have them at the door as people enter or at the door when people leave. If you must pass out a handout during your presentation, tell a joke, talk about last night's game or concert, but do not try to present your presentation. Every eye and mind will be on the handout, not *you*!

Likewise, if there is a commotion or interruption, you may be better off alluding to it and waiting for it to be over than trying to compete with it.

Well, we've covered material that will give you the edge on 93 percent of your presentation. Follow these guidelines and you will convey a confident image even before getting to your content. This information on body language and vocal quality is great. However, if you have nothing worthwhile to say, you can lose your credible image with your audience in about thirty seconds.

So, we're going to take a look at how you can prepare and organize your information in such a way that your audience will change their thinking or be motivated to *do* something, as well as like and accept you.

Content

Keep in mind that there are three basic styles of presenting, and choose the method you feel will most effectively relay your information.

Impromptu (No Preparation)

This is when, without prior warning, someone says to you, "Please come up and *say a few words!*" If you're like me, something in my gut does a nosedive, I suddenly become paralyzed, and not one creative thought enters my mind.

If this happens to you, here is a tip that may at least help you organize your thoughts off the top of your head:

- SAY ——————— Make a statement
- A ——————— Amplify the statement
- FEW——————— Give a few examples
- WORDS ————— Wind it up

Extemporaneous

You use the extemporaneous style when you are well prepared, but your exact words are left to the moment of presentation. This is the method most speakers embrace. They speak from a well-prepared outline from which they have rehearsed. The presentation sounds off the cuff, but adheres to the time limits because of preparation.

Liz Curtis Higgs always appears to be talking without notes, but a closer look reveals that they are in fact in front of her and she refers to them often. "Notes are fine," she says. "Give yourself permission to use them. I very seldom step onto the platform without my notebook full of notes. They are bullet points only. If you know your material (not your *speech*, your *material*— that is, your content), then a bullet point is simply there to remind you what comes next."

I do suggest that you memorize your introduction and conclusion, though, so that you can make genuine eye contact with your audience and sense their feedback. If time goes long and you need to wind it up, you have your conclusion ready so that it stays dynamic and doesn't just piddle out as you slump and say, "I guess that's all I have to say." Yuck!

Manuscript (Completely Written Out and Read)

I must continue quoting Liz on this: "Manuscripts are death. You end up memorizing your presentation, leaving no room for spontaneity or audience interaction. Or worse, you end up reading your speech, leaving no room for eye contact or anything genuine. *Ick!*"

The pitfalls of manuscript speaking include:

- Sounds read

- Hinders rapport

- Lessens eye contact

- Is less rehearsed

If you must speak from a manuscript, try these techniques:

- Triple-space the copy

- Do not staple your pages

- Place pages on right side of podium

- Use paragraph notations or highlight with marker

- Memorize as much as possible

- Don't rely on script too much

- Don't let script interfere with eye contact or pauses

- Try presenting it from an outline

Of the three delivery methods, extemporaneous will work best for you and your audience.

In addition to choosing a delivery method, you will also want to make sure that you know why you are giving your speech. The why of it all is what speech categories are all about. This will help you to research and prepare your remarks and keep you focused on your main purpose.

Purpose Categories

Usually any speech you give will fall into one of the five following categories. It's good to note as you begin your preparation which category your presentation is in so that you can always keep in mind your major purpose.

Inform: You are relaying information so that you impart knowledge. This type tends to include statistics, facts, and interesting data that leads the audience to a certain understanding of your topic.

Entertain: The purpose of this speech is to give pleasure. Its basic tool is humor through storytelling, riddles, and jokes. It is probably one of the most difficult of the five categories to effectively deliver.

Inspire: In the speech to inspire, your main thrust is to encourage and uplift your audience. It's a feel-good presentation that gives hope to the listener.

Convince or Persuade: Here your goal is to change the minds of your audience. You do this, of course, through using techniques common in the speech to inform and the speech to inspire.

Actuate: Your aim is to not only change minds, but to motivate into action. You don't want them just to think differently, you want them to act differently.

Before preparing your content, consider which method of delivery and which purpose category your presentation falls under. This will help you as we go to the next step in preparing and organizing the content.

Preparing Your Presentation

Clark Carlyle, in his book *38 Basic Speech Experiences*, reminds us that "To attempt a speech without preparation is as foolhardy as to attempt to run a marathon without practice."[6] In fact, it is much more difficult to present a well-constructed, well-rehearsed speech than to just get up and ramble on and on. It is said that Woodrow Wilson was once asked to give a five-minute speech, to which he replied, "I'm really not prepared." However, when asked to give a two-hour speech, he jumped right up and said, "Shall I start right now?"

The point, of course, is that speaking concisely and effectively takes a great degree of forethought, research, and rehearsal. The preparation stage is as important as delivering the presentation.

What are the steps involved in preparation? Let me outline them in the order you should follow.

Choose a topic: Sometimes you will be given one; other times you will be allowed free rein to choose your own topic. If possible, choose to speak on something that you are passionate about. Author and master presenter Florence Littauer emphasizes the importance of speaking from the heart: "When I speak from personal experience about something that is dear to me, I don't even need notes!"

Comedienne Kay DeKalb Smith suggests using relevant topics that are laced with humor and honesty. "People respond to common ground experiences—pantyhose, carpooling, and car washes. I try to choose topics that relate to things that people go through—of course, always with a sparkling dash of humor!" I might add—even hilarity!

Brainstorm: Carol Kent says she writes down "everything I already know about the topic I'm working on. Then I write down every resource I know of that will give me additional information—books, people, articles, and organizations." Remember that in a brainstorm there are no rules; enjoy the freedom of jotting down even the ridiculous in hopes that a thread of a great idea will surface.

Narrow the scope of your topic: Carol Kent again: "I usually have too much material before I come up with my outline points—so I write out an aim by finishing this sentence: 'What do I want my audience/reader to *do* as a result of hearing/reading this message?' If I feel that my response is too vague, I add the question, 'By doing what?' Any extra point that doesn't fit my aim gets eliminated."

Choose three main points to discuss: One helpful rule of thumb is to limit your main points to perhaps three ideas. You can't talk about all the effects of world hunger in fifteen minutes, but you can talk about three ways that your audience can assist in feeding the hungry in one small village in South Africa.

Limiting the scope of your ideas helps you keep within your time constraints. Using more main points will force you to be very creative in keeping your audience with you.

Research

Today the Internet has opened to us almost more avenues of research than we can bear. Blend this with interviews and life experience, and your presentation begins to take shape. Some presenters, like Florence Littauer, read a daily newspaper from a major city and keep front-cover stories from noted magazines. Florence takes the cover off the magazine and staples the lead story to it so that at a glance she can grab the story she wants to draw from. As an example, she showed me at least eight covers of *Time* on which Ross Perot was the cover story. It was an interesting commentary simply to see which picture they printed of him and what the headline read.

As Christians, we must not bury our heads in the sand and be ignorant of what's going on in the world around us. If you're really serious about being an effective presenter, your best research can take place on a daily basis as you collect stories and statistics that will contribute to the enhancement of your information.

Thesis

Oops. Sorry to drop an old writing term in your lap. However, it's really the best word I can find to describe the next important step in your preparation process. Technically a thesis is a proposition, statement, or assertion that is to be proved or discussed. It is the *why* of your speech. Just as we saw the importance of creating your Reason for Writing statement, you must clearly articulate your Purpose for Presenting. It's necessary to make this statement at the very beginning of the preparation process since everything you include in the following outline must align itself naturally under this idea.

In speaking, however, I do not suggest that you begin with "The purpose of my presentation is to—" Boring! In fact, you should write your introduction only *after* you have outlined your presentation and even written your conclusion. The Purpose statement is just for your working outline.

Outline

Once you've gathered all of your research data and have a purpose in mind, it's time to get those ideas on paper in an order that makes sense. Like brainstorming, your first outline can go crazy with listing your three main points and all of the ideas that come under them. Congratulations. You have now successfully created a ten-hour speech! So, just as in weeding a garden, you must go back to the full outline and decide what can be pulled and what can stay. You may even continue to cut things as you rehearse if they seem to stray down a bunny path or force you over your time limit.

Can you believe that we've spent this much time talking strategy, but have yet to actually create our presentation? My personal preference is to spend half of my preparation time on research and organizing, one fourth of my time creating the actual presentation, and one fourth of my time rehearsing it. Again, it's spending time sharpening the saw: "If I had eight hours to chop down a tree, I'd spend six hours sharpening an axe."[7]

Putting All the Pieces Together

It's important at this point to determine what your time constraints are. This will help you decide how much information to cover under each point. Here is a guideline that may help:

- •Fifteen-minute speech

    Introduction—1.5 minutes

    Point #1—4 minutes

    Point #2—4 minutes

    Point #3—4 minutes

    Conclusion—1.5 minutes

- • Forty-minute speech

    Introduction—2 minutes

    Point #1—13 minutes

    Point #2—13 minutes

    Point #3—13 minutes

    Conclusion—2 minutes

Adhering to this time frame will help you keep your points balanced and fairly discussed. It also serves as a natural breakdown of a major goal into smaller steps to accomplish the goal.

Basically there are three pieces to your presentation: the Introduction, the Body, and the Conclusion. If you know the final destination of your speaking journey, you can write the conclusion first. However, sometimes it takes careful planning and rehearsing of the body for it to naturally emerge from your material. For the sake of following the final chronological path of the presentation, we will be discussing these areas in the order you will present them.

As you look at the nuts and bolts of the how-to portion of this chapter that we are delving into next, let me challenge you to keep in mind Proverbs 12:25: "An anxious heart weighs a man down, but a kind word cheers him up." And, "Pleasant words are a honeycomb, sweet to the soul and healing to the bones" (Prov. 16:24). As speakers, we hold the keys of cheerfulness and healing. What an awesome responsibility.

Nuts and Bolts

While Being Introduced

Remember that the image you convey begins even before you are introduced and begin to speak. In fact, it's very important that during your introduction you realize that the audience will divide its attention between the person introducing you and how you are responding. Here are several suggestions to follow during your introduction:

Sit tall in your chair. This may be the time you want to tense and relax muscles or practice breathing properly from the diaphragm and abdomen to slow your heart rate and lengthen your breathing pattern.

Give the introducer your full attention. If you look out the window or talk to the person next to you, so will the members of your audience. They will likely mirror your behavior even before you take the stage.

Rid yourself of distractions such as pens, loose change, paper clips, unnecessary notes, and any other clutter.

After the introduction, don't meander to the podium, but jump up as your name is being said and walk quickly with purpose and enthusiasm to the podium.

Take a few moments in silence to place your notes where you want them (it would be better to already have them in place before the introduction) and adjust the microphone. Now, take a deep breath, smile, and enjoy a few seconds of the Golden Pause before you deliver your first words.

Concentrate on making eye contact and slowing down your rate of speech as you deliver your first well-prepared, well-rehearsed, and memorized opening words.

The Introduction

Keeping in mind that you will want to write this last and memorize it for your presentation, let's take a look at the importance of your introductory words and ways you can grab the attention of your audience.

The function or purpose of your introduction can be remembered by the acronym CAP: You want to establish

Common Ground

Authority

Profit value

Wow! What can you say that will embody all of these elements? Do *not* begin on a negative note and *never* apologize. People don't really care that you missed your last flight or your throat hurts or you didn't have time to prepare. Remember that you need to say something positive and invigorating that will get and maintain their attention. Master presenter and Bible teacher Millie Dienert reminds us that the introduction is "building a bridge" between us and our audience. Here are some ideas:

- Humorous anecdote

- Related illustration ("The best speaker is he who turns ears into eyes." Arab Proverb)

- Series of thought-provoking questions

- Reference to music, occasion, or problem

- Interesting description

- Shocking statement

- Quotation

- Rhetorical question

- List of statistics

- Visual aid

Jesus was a master storyteller, and we can learn much about His effectiveness as a public speaker by reading His parables. Carol Kent says that "stories are definitely the most effective speaking tool. In the postmodern world people are used to receiving information in sound bites—TV, and in visually graphic form. They have short attention spans. Stories (personal illustrations) that make truth memorable capture the attention of the audience and help them to understand the point we're making. If you wrap a truth or biblical principle in a great story, people will never forget it!"

I hope your mind is beginning to overflow with wonderful and innovative ways you can introduce your topic. We just needed to get your creative juices flowing. The introduction is supposed to bait the audience so you can hook 'em. However, it's the body of your presentation that reels them in!

The Body

You will want to pick a strategy for organizing the body of your presentation so that your preparation goes smoothly. It's *so* important to come up with, well, let me call it a *gimmick,* so that your audience will not only be interested enough to listen, but will remember the main points. Remember, most people forget 50 to 75 percent of what they've heard within forty-eight hours. What a challenge for us as we deliberately create something memorable.

Just as we map our vacation to figure out exactly how we're going to get from Six Flags to King's Island, we must develop a speaking outline that logically leads the listener from one point to the next. Here are some of my favorites:

Acronyms: Can you remember what the acronym CAP stands for? I could create a whole presentation from the three main points Common Ground, Authority, and Profit Value. Using these as the main points of the body helps the listener remember them since the first letters spell a word. Wouldn't it be great to come up with an acronym for the humane society that spelled the word CATS? I *love* it.

Alliteration: Later in the section on goal setting, I try to create a new way for you to remember the three steps to attaining your dreams. So, in my three main points I used the repetition of a consonant sound: Ponder, Plan, and Proceed. And, for those of you who enjoy literary symbolism, I have just successfully used foreshadowing—planting an idea that will eventually be discussed.

Questions: Think about some thought-provoking questions that can tease the listener into anticipating your answers. For instance, a great outline for the body of a speech to youth might be these three questions: Where do you want to go? How are you going to get there? When are you going to begin?

Verbs: Especially effective in a presentation where you want to motivate into action (the speech to actuate), choose strong action words as your main points: "Ready, Set, Go!" might work. Or, in a sales situation, repeat the same verb: "Sell, Sell, Sell!" using different techniques for selling your product behind each point.

Journalistic technique: Remember the "who, what, when, where, why, and how" questions? Use these as your main points and you've also employed the use of alliteration. Save the last punch with the "how" and you've covered everything on your topic and provided a dynamic challenge at the end.

Chronological or experiential order: This works best in a testimonial or retelling a life story. Simply pull out the most important aspects and tell them in the order they occurred such as "Past, Present, and Future" or "Step 1, Step 2, and Step 3."

There are certain strategies that a debate team employs as it argues its case. These also make excellent organizational strategies as you prepare and present the body of your presentation:

Problem/solution: If your topic forces you to address a problem and outline some solutions, follow these steps and your speech is practically written for you:

- Focus on the problem

- Present the need

- Satisfy the need

- Visualize the end results so that your audience can "see" the solution

- Stir into action

Cause/effect: If you are giving an information speech addressing serious consequences or effects, use examples of how certain causes are leading to either damaging or positive effects. Perhaps the athletic department has had to cut the girls' softball program for lack of funds. You could outline the three main causes for the program being cut and the adverse effects that the school and children will suffer if the cut should go through.

Advantage/disadvantage: It may work to organize your topic by discussing the advantages and disadvantages. If you feel that the implementation of the idea is overall advantageous to adopt, make that your last point.

Escalating: Organize your points on a type of scale:

- Small to large

- Easy to hard

- Inexpensive to costly

In addition to these outlining suggestions, I like what author and leadership mentor Fred Smith calls the "Combination of Three," which helps to flesh out your outlined points. When I think of my locker combination, I think of the three numbers that open the door. In this case, the combination opens the minds of our audience. Fred's "combination" is

- Point

- Story

- Essence (statement)

He introduces his point and tells a story that illustrates the point. Then he summarizes the point in an "essence statement," which sometimes reads like the "moral of the story" from the old fables.

"Point, story, statement." It's a great bodybuilding strategy.

Also, like Fred, if you can use humor or the element of surprise, your audience will remember your points. Fred jokes that "Moses was the first to break all Ten Commandments." Then he quips, "Too many marriages start out in bliss and end up in blisters!" He loves to come up with memorable phrases: "The fallacy of fantasy."[8] You get the idea. When you use colorful descriptions and choose words that conjure up mental pictures, it's more likely that your audience will not only hear your message, but will see it and remember it.

The Conclusion

People remember most what they hear last, so this is where you want to pack your biggest punch.

I would suggest keeping *under* your time limit. You want to stop speaking *before* the audience stops listening. If you sense through feedback from people that they are tired of listening and have tuned you out, you're better off to deliver your well-prepared and rehearsed conclusion and stop their agony. There is some wisdom in the advice "Get up, speak up, and shut up!" "Know when to quit—even when people seem to want you to go on!" master communicator Millie Dienert says.

Your conclusion does not need to be long—perhaps only 5 percent of your total time allotment. Deliver it with confidence and finality. Stay at the podium for several seconds after delivering the final statement implementing the use of the Golden Pause. This allows the idea to sink it. Do not bring up any new material or concepts at this time. Tie up loose ends and repeat power statements.

As with the introduction, you can choose from a variety of options for your last "memorable mouthful!"

- Use a quotable quote

- Give a dynamic challenge

- Outline again your plan of action

- Ask a thought-provoking question

- Summarize the main points

- Make a statement of personal intention

- Provide an illustration by ending with a key story

Remember the statistics? During your first thirty seconds, 25 percent of the audience liked you, 25 percent did not, and 50 percent were taking a "wait and see attitude." You have a great opportunity in your *last* thirty seconds to turn the tide of opinion in your favor so that almost 100 percent feel that you have given them something of value to take away with them.

Rehearsal

This is the area that, frankly, can be very boring and time consuming for the would-be speaker. However, it is often in the area of rehearsal that sets apart the really fine speakers from the could-be speakers.

Don't get me wrong. There is value in looking over your notes ahead of time and even giving your speech to yourself "in your head." However, to perfect timing, delivery, and word choice, you *must* spend adequate time in rehearsal if you want to be the best you can be. Here are some hints:

Rehearse out loud: This will help perfect your timing, assist you in choosing the right words and power phrases, and help you to gain confidence since you've given it a trial run.

Overpractice: Overpracticing will also enforce the strengths of your presentation and help you to gain confidence for the final presentation.

Stand in front of a mirror: If you practice in front of a mirror, you will see just how much eye contact you are making and be able to evaluate the effectiveness of your facial expressions.

Tape-record your voice: This is the best way for you to determine whether you are speaking at the proper rate of speed, allowing for voice fluctuation and a confident tone.

Videotape your presentation, then critique it: Are you using enough gestures? How's your posture? Can they see your knees shaking? The video can sometimes be your best friend, proving that some of the things we feel are not even seen by the audience!

Try out your presentation and ideas on family members and friends: Now, don't just practice on your mom, who thinks you're perfect, or someone who doesn't have a clue as to what good speaking entails! Go for honest feedback on everything from your content to body language.

Concentrate on your subject matter so that you are not distracted: When I was taking theater classes in college, the professor stressed the importance of concentrating so much that we could not forget lines or get sidetracked. Concentration demands total focus on what you are saying and how you are saying it. Effective speakers learn what to block out and what to invite into their presentation.

Practice it in your mind: This story was printed in the late 1970s in the *Jackson Citizen Patriot* magazine supplement and came out of the Vietnam War. Apparently a soldier, wounded in battle, was bedridden on his back for an extended amount of time from a back injury.

While recovering, he was *totally* bored. It occurred to him that he had always wanted to learn to type and wondered if there was a way to use his time productively. Someone on the base found a typing manual and taped a photograph of the keyboard above him so that he could look at the home keys and, in his mind, practice typing.

Once he was recovered enough to sit up, they brought a typewriter in and can you believe it? He typed thirty words per minute having never placed a finger on the home keys before! See what power our minds can have in assisting us in preparing our presentation?

Visualize yourself in the speaking hall and imagine the sounds and feel from the audience: There is seldom a day that goes by that I do not see myself in my mind's eye standing on the stage as the hostess of TimeOut for Women! I imagine the sounds, the temperature, the smells, and the sights of the arena so that each day I get more and more comfortable standing, speaking, and singing before thousands of women.

If you do know what your presentation area looks like, imagine yourself there and rehearse what you are going to say—in your mind—as you imagine how it will feel to present at that location. You will have so much more confidence when the real thing gets there!

Time your rehearsals and highlight places in your outline you can cut if the real thing goes long: Again, it may be good to enlist the help of a friend or fellow presenter who can time your presentation and make sure that you leave your audience with the strongest message possible.

Extensive preparation leads to self-confidence which leads to audience interest which leads to audience participation which leads to an *accomplished objective*. If you know your subject and speak from your heart as if you mean it, you *will do great*.

Remember the Be's of public speaking:

- Be enthusiastic

- Be sincere

- Be trustworthy

- Be prepared

- Be confident

- Be early

- Be conscious of feedback

Polishing your platform performance may be the very thing that leads you into a leadership position. And once you've achieved a level of leadership, the effectiveness of your public speaking skills is exactly what will keep you effective in that role.

More important than the words we speak, however, is the condition of our hearts, for what is inside us will surely overflow from us. In Matthew 12:34 Jesus stated, "For out of the overflow of the heart the mouth speaks." We do and become what we think about. This is why it is so important for us, before we even put a foot on that platform, to prepare our hearts so that God's truths can flow through a clean vessel.

"Finally, brothers [and sisters], whatever is true, whatever is noble, whatever is right, whatever is pure, whatever is lovely, whatever is admirable—if anything is excellent or praiseworthy—think about such things" (Phil. 4:8).

Well, perhaps this discussion of how to speak in front of people has really stressed you out. Your heart does a pittypat, but you're excited to put into practice these techniques. We've covered some ways for you to deal with performance anxiety, but there are other things that stress you too, aren't there? Don't you wonder how Jesus handled stress?

Next we're going to take a look at what causes stress in our lives (other than getting up in front of people), the consequences of stress, and how we can successfully deal with stress the way Jesus did.

*L*ord, *please encourage my dear sister that she can work through her fears and serve You faithfully in the places You have placed her to lead. Give her the confidence she needs to step out of her comfort zone and boldly show others the way—Your way. Amen.*

six

How to Not Stress in a
Stressed-out World

Y ou are truly unusual if you haven't been overwhelmed by stress or felt the debilitating crush of depression in your life. Those diabolical twins get most of us at one time or another.

Fighting to keep a peaceful mind in a chaotic world is a battle indeed. It's a common problem that everyone complains about and savvy businessmen have tried to cash in on. Advice on how to cope has filled pages of countless books, and devices from solid maple massage tools to bottled concoctions that carry hefty price tags line store shelves.

How do you cope with stress?

I like to visit our local drugstore and sort through the vast array of greeting cards. Among my favorites is a card with a caricature of a kitty sitting in a bathtub. The caption reads: "When life gets too hectic, I've always found that a nice hot bath can solve most problems."

Inside, the card reads: "I've been here since last Thursday..."

One of our TimeOut staff members has this sign hanging above her desk: "Anti-stress kit." Within a huge circle about the size of a cantaloupe are the words "BANG HEAD HERE." As if that weren't clear enough, the instructions below read:

1. Place on FIRM surface

2. Follow directions provided in the circle on the front of the kit

3. Repeat until you are anti-stressed or become unconscious

Then there's the *Peanuts* cartoon. Sitting on top of his doghouse, Snoopy is reading his expectations as the boss while Woodstock sits at the typewriter: "This next list will have the names of ten million dogs. I need a detailed report on each dog's activities typed up in triplicate." Dazed, Woodstock spins off the doghouse and klunks to the ground headfirst. Snoopy: "I hate it when my secretary faints!"

Recently, while gathering some materials at an office supply store, I glanced across the aisle and noticed several pads and calendars packaged together. One notepad read: "Stress (n.) A condition. When a person's mind overcomes the body's desire to choke the living daylights out of someone who desperately deserves it." Scribbled across the top of another notepad was: "Panic, Stress, Chaos: Just Another Routine Day." Then a Shakespeare-looking sketch with the words: "To do or not to do. (A little editorial liberty.)" Finally: "Things I should have done yesterday," with "ToDoCanDoMustDo-DeepDo." Enough said.

How do you cope with stress? Perhaps the better question is, How did Jesus cope with stress? Let's take a look at what stress is, what causes it, and some human remedies for it. Then we'll look at how the Master Himself dealt with it.

Stress has been defined as "the external demands of life and the internal attitudes and thoughts that require us to adapt, adjust, or conform." In other words, coping with stress often requires us to change, and most people resist change.

Causes of Stress

Research points to five main causes of stress in today's culture. The first is a change in the way we live. Today, we live nomadic lives. Gone are the days when grandpa, brothers and sisters, uncles, aunts, and a few cousins worked side-by-side in the family business or as a team farming the family land. Not long ago when a son got married, his dad portioned off a parcel of land where the son and new wife began their life together, close to family and a loving support group. Neighbors joined together building each other's barns and taking turns working on each other's quilts. A sense of community, familiarity, and history were vital to their lives.

Christian family therapist Dr. Samuel Roth says that more than 20 percent of the population in the United States moves each year, which creates an incredible amount of added stress in our lives. Like a plant torn from the ground and replanted in a new garden every spring, this is unsettling and takes its toll. We feel this stress even if we are not the ones moving, but lose a dear friend or neighbor to a new job in a new city. Deep and lasting friendships don't have a chance to grow, a sense of continuity and security ends up missing from many lives. In fact, moving involves a grieving process and deep feelings of loss.

The second major cause of stress is financial struggles. Many marital arguments and family breakups are caused by the financial strain involved in family relationships. As a college administrator, I was painfully aware of the debt the graduates owed as they crossed the platform to receive their diplomas: "Mike, $25,000, Jenny, $42,500, Sarah, $12,500," and so on as the names droned on. Many, if they get a job, know that their first year's salary likely won't even match what they owe in school bills. Add this indebtedness to a new marriage where couples may then disagree on how to spend money, and stress compounds itself.

Reason number three is that there is just too much to do and not enough time to do it. Expectations are way beyond what can easily and realistically be accomplished. We live in a fast-paced world where we hear the female blues singer gravel: "I can bring home the bacon, fry it up in a pan, and never ever let you forget you're a man . . . I'm a woman. . . ." Well, you get the idea. We think we have to do it all, so we easily overcommit to the point where we can't do anything well or enjoy it. And too many of us think this is expected of us.

Unresolved relational issues is number four on the list. Come with me each morning to the local coffee shop I visit and eavesdrop on any conversation and the major topic is *always* hurt over a relationship. "My son didn't send a Mother's Day card to me." "My sister doesn't talk with me since my brother and I placed Mom in a nursing home." "I wish my husband would stop divorce proceedings and move home." "My neighbor will never accept an invitation from me to have lunch." "That man actually insulted me because of my new hair style!" Women, especially, are vulnerable to this stress because we place such a high value on our relationships. We like all the ends tied up and everyone happy. This leads to the next stressor. . . .

Trying to control someone else's attitudes, behavior, or responses is number five. Dr. Roth reminds us that "we can be responsive to, but not responsible for another individual." Trying to maintain control over another human being only adds to our unresolved relational issues and our frustration at feeling out of control.

If you think that we are alone in facing these stresses, just take a quick overview of the life that Jesus led. He faced each stress that we do. When He was an infant, His parents were uprooted and forced to flee into Egypt so that Herod would not kill Him. We even get the impression that during His adult ministry He did not have permanent roots: "The Son of Man has no place to lay his head (Matt. 8:20).

We don't have details about Jesus' financial situation, but we do know that Judas, who held the books, was not honest in his dealings. In fact, John 12:4-6 reveals that he regularly helped himself to the cash—embezzling money from God!

Jesus also knew the stress of having too much to do and not enough time to do it in. No matter where He was, the crowds gathered and pressed in upon Him for healing, teaching, and advice. There were always things left undone . . . just not enough time!

Think of the unresolved relational issues that faced Him. His own neighbors did not understand or believe in him. Matthew 13:54-58 recounts Jesus visiting His hometown and teaching in the synagogue. The people were amazed, but also offended. Jesus commented that "only in his hometown and in his own house is a prophet without honor" (v. 57). Even Jesus suffered the hurt incurred through relationships!

Finally, Jesus, too, was faced with wanting to change people's hearts, only to have them hardened. Mark 3:5 records that "He looked around at them in anger and, deeply distressed at their stubborn hearts." Even after walking out to His own disciples on the water, Mark 6:52 records that "their hearts were hardened." These were men who had experienced His miracles and holy teaching! Think of how we would feel if we faced the same opposition!

Well, we want to look at how Jesus handled these stresses as well as many other things, but first, let's look at some models that can help us keep our stress under control.

Circles of Influence

Years ago I came across a diagram that has helped put things in perspective for me when I get stressed over things out of my control. I don't know its source, but it has been a constant encouragement to me for over two decades. It is called "Circles of Influence" and is made up of three circles. The bull's-eye in the middle represents the things I can control. The next circle outside of that represents things that I have some influence over. The last—and I might add the largest—circle represents the things that I neither control nor influence.

When facing a stressful situation, it's helpful to analyze which circle the stressor falls within.

Fred Smith, who has been a mentor to my husband and me for over twenty-five years, told us a story not uncommon today. He was one of two hundred passengers buckled in their seats ready for takeoff when the pilot announced that due to a maintenance problem, the plane would be grounded for at least four hours until the problem was fixed.

As you can imagine, every kind of reaction erupted throughout the air bus: shouting, swearing, fists pounding briefcases, and general chaos. As Fred looked around at the commotion taking place, he asked himself which circle of influence this situation fell under. Being the genius that he is, he quickly came to the conclusion that this situation was out of his circle of control and influence.

Angry passengers filed out. Fred looked at his briefcase loaded with piles of unfinished work, glanced at the now quiet and empty plane, accepted a cup of fresh hot coffee from the smiling flight attendant, and dug into the briefcase. No phone, no interruptions, and a bottomless coffee cup allowed him to maximize to his advantage a situation out of his control. He enjoyed getting more work done than he could possibly have accomplished in his office.

"God often comforts us; not by changing the circumstances of our lives, but by changing our attitudes towards them."[1]

Reactions to Stress

Our reaction to stress usually falls into one of three categories.

Internalize Stress

Sometimes we internalize it, which is dangerous because an emotional response (such as anger) often becomes physical. If we keep "stuffing" stress down inside, we most likely will end up suffering:

- Increased heart rate
- Increased perspiration
- Tensed muscles
- Increased production of fat and sugar
- Increased chemicals in the bloodstream
- Increased hormones and adrenaline
- Migraine headaches
- Mood swings

- Aches and pains

- Depression

Let me touch on a very emotional and sensitive issue for a moment. According to my friend Sue Liljenberg, the organizer of a ministry called Healing Hearts, which assists postabortive women in their emotional and spiritual healing, almost 48 percent of women in the United States have had abortions. Ramah and Mourning Joy, two other such groups, confirm this shocking statistic. Many women leave the clinic with only this advice: "Pretend that this never happened—it's only fetal tissue—and don't tell anyone."

Twenty years later, a woman becomes very depressed for apparently no reason. Then she begins to suffer migraines and new aches. She goes to a medical doctor who doesn't discover any physical explanation for her symptoms. On the way home from the doctor's office she listens to her local Christian radio station where the song "A Baby's Prayer" is being sung by Kathy Troccoli. The woman begins sobbing uncontrollably and has to pull off the side of the road as finally she deals with the grief and guilt of her past situation.

A postabortive woman may not always respond in this way, but we've seen it so many times and know that internalizing this kind or any kind of stress will not stay buried forever. At some time it will erupt, and often at a high cost.

Act It Out

If we don't internalize it, we might act it out. Women have been known to act out stress through an eating disorder or even having an affair. Then there's the woman who goes on a spending binge.

The wife of my son's Little League coach got caught in this trap. She was actually chemically depressed and didn't realize it until she ran up every credit card to its limit in one month's time. She was burying her emotional pain for a few moments that the spending high would give her, but by the time she drove into her driveway she was more depressed than ever because she didn't know how they would pay for her expenditures! Through some good counseling she dealt with some painful past issues and was able to put a freeze on spending.

Talk It Out

Some of us talk it out. Of course, this is the most appropriate way to deal with stress. The best place to begin the talking-out process is in prayer to our Heavenly Father. Jesus, in John 14:13-14, tells us, "And I will do whatever you ask in my name, so that the Son may bring glory to the Father. You may ask me for anything in my name, and I will do it."

I highly recommend Christian counseling, pastoral guidance, and support from a trusted friend during the talking-out process, but as we've seen so many times, all of the sincere listening hearts in the world cannot heal our deeply inflicted wounds—only the supernatural power and grace of a loving Heavenly Father.

Bottled-up stress will present itself in some outward form, so it's better to choose the most healthy approach and talk it out.

Destressing Without Distress

Even though it seems we live in an out-of-control world that adds to our stress, there are several ways that we can better manage and control what *is* in our circle of influence.

The first is to set our priorities and achieve balance in our lives. We can develop and expand our spiritual dimension by reading the Bible, praying, and consciously obeying God's Word.

Bible Study

In preparation for writing and speaking engagements over the years, I've developed a personal Bible study system that might work for you too. Although it took three years, I finally made it through the *One-Year Bible*! The reason it took me so long is that I didn't just want to read to cover a certain number of pages. I wanted to read to gather Spirit-led information that would assist me in my personal spiritual journey and in encouraging others in theirs.

Whether I have just five minutes, fifty, or a whole day to spend in the Word, I use the same method. First, I pray. I don't usually pray *for* anything or anybody until after my study. I just ask God to reveal to me new truths in His Word this day. I ask for clarity of mind and focus and a sensitive spirit to His.

I always keep a set of 3-by-5 cards, a highlighter, and a pen nearby. When a thought hits me or a verse touches me, I highlight the passage in my Bible and write it down on the card. I then write the Bible reference on the top left side of the card.

On the top right side of the card I assign a topic. For instance, Exodus 34:6-7 describes God as being compassionate, slow to anger, abounding in love, and forgiving. So, I write *God* in the upper right-hand corner.

I keep these cards in a 3-by-5 file holder that can probably accommodate over two thousand cards. If I don't already have a category set up, I take an index divider and label it *God* and file my card behind it. I also enjoy using Matthew Henry's commentaries, the *Quest Study Bible*, and the *NIV Study Bible* when I need clarification or more information on a topic.

From experience, I know that this is an effective way for me to study: I've read the information, thought about it, written it down, and filed it for future reference. When I want to write a song or give a presentation on God's character, I simply reference that section in my card file, put the cards in the order I plan to discuss them, and begin work.

There may be some computer software that also assists in this type of study, but for this old high school English teacher, the old research paper method works best. It allows me to actively participate in the exciting discovery of God's truths and organize the ideas for future reference.

Setting Goals

Setting goals that are realistic for this season of your life will decrease your stress. Remember that we may understand God's call, or purpose, in one season of life, prepare for it in another, and see its fulfillment yet in a later season. In my twenties, I was mistaken in thinking that I was to somehow save the whole high school where I was teaching single-handedly, have a perfectly clean house with perfectly behaved toddlers, while carrying four different class preparations, five extracurricular activities, plus involvement in a weekend music ministry!

As my son's first birthday approached, I remember not feeling well. In fact, I was sure that I was running a fever. But my parents were visiting from out of town to celebrate, so we packed up Steve and his soon-to-be-four-year-old sister and had birthday cake at a restaurant that gave out free birthday cakes! (We were, you know, on a very tight budget!)

By the time I went to bed on Saturday evening I was really really tired and hot. Maybe a good night's sleep would help. Well, my night's sleep lasted until Sunday night when I woke up hallucinating with a 105-degree fever!

When my husband, Paul, discovered how seriously ill I was, he called our family physician, who was also a fellow church member. Howard sent me directly to the hospital. For close to a week I lay in that hospital bed dehydrated, losing weight, and running a fever that no medication could break. I lay there literally thanking the Lord that it looked like I would probably die that week! I was so miserable trying to live my whole life in one season that I was depressed and ready to go home to Jesus.

I'm almost embarrassed now to tell you, but while I could hardly think straight, I started thanking God that my kids were so young that they probably wouldn't remember or miss me too much when I was gone, and that Paul was young enough to find another real nice wife who could do better than me.

Well, Thursday morning I was saved from exploratory surgery when I woke with absolutely no fever. I was a little bummed because dying and going to heaven seemed like such an easy way to deal with all of my stress, but I knew that if God allowed me to live, it was because He was teaching me something and had a greater purpose in my life.

I cannot stand before you today and say that I always set realistic goals for myself. Many will tell you that I've really bitten off a big bite as we've expanded the TimeOut for Women! ministry, but now my staff and I do make a conscious effort to keep my goals on a realistic time line and to enlist help or delegate when possible.

Balancing Demands

To combat stress, we must also find ways to accomplish and balance the demands of our jobs, our homes, and our families. I used to teach from a booklet titled *The Tyranny of the Urgent*. I chose it not only because it embodied great writing elements, but because it gave me a chance to discuss with high school students the difference between what is urgent and what is important.

We often forfeit doing what is really important to us because we feel we have to put out fires and deal with the emergencies that come our way. We must ask, "Why am I fighting this battle if it isn't important to me? What *should* I be spending my time on?"

If raising my children is the most important value in my life right now, why am I working a meaningless job, forty hours per week, that prevents me from involvement in my priority? If ministering through music is a priority with me, why am I volunteering at the hospital instead? If I want more time alone with my husband, why do I feel pressured to accept social invitations that bore me?

Not too long ago a television magazine profiled a family with two working parents and two boys under the age of five. The parents worked different shifts in hopes that the children would have to spend less time at day care.

After the reporter documented the extra costs involved in a household with a working mom, they discovered that with the out-to-eat expenses, gas to her job, day care, and "guilt gifts," that it was actually costing them around $2,000 per year for the mom to work outside the home.

All of that time and sacrifice they thought they were making to get ahead financially was actually putting them in the hole. By quitting her job (for the time) and performing the tasks that she had previously hired out, the mom benefited by being able to raise her boys, spend time with her husband, and save $2,000 per year!

We also discovered after my near-death experience that my working was not financially productive, emotionally uplifting, or medically wise. For a few years after that, I clipped coupons, cooked economically, sewed most of our clothing, and found ways to make it financially possible to raise my kids in a loving, relaxed atmosphere. You'll get an earful about day care from our kids even today. They are so grateful that we had those years together.

To stave off stress, it's important to make time for a vacation, hobby, and recreation. The old saying "All work and no play makes Jack a dull boy" is only partially true. It also makes Jack a less rested and more stressed boy. When God created the heavens and the earth, He rested on the seventh day. Now, it seems to me that God, in all of His power, didn't really need the rest, but He wanted to set an example for us that vacations and time off are necessary to us physically, emotionally, and spiritually.

We live about forty-five minutes from Lake Michigan. We've found that after a long, stressful day, if we pack a picnic or eat at an outdoor cafe on the beach to watch the sunset, we feel refreshed and as if we've been away for days. It's pretty cheap stress therapy. Not everyone lives near a Great Lake, but every city or town has charming and soothing places to visit. I once read a magazine article that actually suggested that doing housework can be relaxing. The writer maintained that performing routine, repetitive actions such as ironing, folding clothes, or sweeping a floor actually help reduce stress.

I've also been told that some of the "no-brainer" activities stimulate the right side of the brain in creating and problem solving. Come to think of it, I've created the hook line (the theme and most memorable and repeated line) of several songs while putting laundry in the dryer or mowing the yard. Perhaps my lack of creativity is a direct result of how little I've been cleaning. A dirty house must represent a noncreative day for me.

Preparing for the Unexpected

Another stress buster is to prepare for the unexpected. (Hope for the best; prepare for the worst.) We must also accept what is out of our control.

In 1983 my husband served as the vice president of an oil company. That year the company tapped the largest gas well ever discovered in the state. It didn't take long for the owners to realize that they were financially set for the rest of their lives, so why should they keep twenty-some employees, an office, and go to work anymore?

One by one, all were forced to step out of the business with no place to go. The employees were not given a severance package, and we had few resources. For months we prayed that a job would open in the city where we lived, but God turned a silent ear toward us. Every day for the six months he had no work, my husband would go to church first thing and kneel at the altar. He placed a situation that was out of our control in the hands of the Master who does control.

It was a tough time, but we know now that God was testing our faith and preparing our hearts for an even more traumatic financial devastation that would hit us in 1990. This time we were faced with four years of unemployment! But rather than looking back at that time as depressing and stressful, I remember the faithfulness and grace of God as He provided and saw us through. Sometimes stress is a conduit to peace and joy!

Job loss, illness, death, and the behavior of someone else are things that are out of our control. What we can control is *who* we turn to. If I acknowledge that God is in control and sees the situation from start to finish, I put my trust in Him and rest without stress.

Coping with Disappointment

Another way to get the best of stress is to find ways to cope with disappointment. One way to do this is through positive self-talk and prayer.

When in 1990 we found ourselves without work, my husband's self-esteem plummeted. Even though out of 105 oil companies, only five survived oil plunging to eight dollars per barrel, he fought blaming himself and looking back wondering if there were something he could have done to avoid this disaster.

We both found that he had better days when we practiced positive self-talk, such as, "I still have qualities that are valuable. We have wonderful friends praying for us. This is a devastating situation, but we'll get through it. I have worth and value."

Of course, our greatest strength and encouragement came through the Lord as we daily, sometimes hourly, committed the situation to Him. He gave us that peace that passes all understanding!

Learning to Be Flexible

It was Sir Walter Scott who said, "The willow which bends to the tempest often escapes better than the oak which resists it." Being flexible means giving up some control, but sometimes that works to our advantage.

One of my first teaching assignments was to organize the journalism class so that we could produce a weekly high school newspaper. Until I was hired, journalism was viewed as an easy A for which students didn't have to work. It was a sixth-hour class, so many a student signed up, thinking she or he could cut class everyday.

For a few weeks, I tried every teaching strategy in the book to motivate each student to participate. I tried to rigidly fit this group into a textbook, inflexibly following it to the letter. Being new, I didn't want the students to think that I wasn't in control, but it was so obvious that I wasn't, that one day, I finally gave in.

I told the students that I was giving up complete control over the newspaper and it was their responsibility to figure out how the thirty of them could divide up the work and successfully produce a weekly paper. I turned to the five most unlikely "leaders" and said, "This week, you will be the lead editorial staff and you will be responsible for organizing the class with titles and assignments so we, for once, meet deadline."

After their mouths closed and they could see straight again, what happened was amazing. By Tuesday they had identified titles and responsibilities, brainstormed article ideas, and given out assignments. By Wednesday articles began rolling in, and the typesetting began. By Thursday the editorial staff was wearing ties and power suits, and by Friday, our first edition hit the cafeteria and was a rousing success!

The classroom took on a relaxed buzz everyday and was quite organized even though no one sat in an assigned seat. There were few tardies, no skips, and not one discipline issue. Once I learned to be flexible and relinquish a little control, we never missed a deadline. We all learned to go with the flow. And my headaches finally subsided.

Always Have a Plan B

You may remember, as I do, watching the presidential candidates campaigning for the 1996 election. In a very moving presentation on live television before millions of viewers, Elizabeth Dole was introduced to the Republican convention. Rather than standing on the platform and speaking behind the podium, she walked right down to the floor of the arena to talk face-to-face and personally with her audience.

Not too far into her presentation, her hand-held microphone suddenly gave out, which is not uncommon. Did she panic? There was only a moment's interruption as, unruffled, she handed the microphone to a production person and lifted the spare microphone out of its cradle. She never skipped a beat (even though I'm sure the heart of the producer did for a moment!)

They had hoped for the best, but anticipated the worst, and had plan B at the ready.

Develop a Positive Attitude:

Attitude is a choice. Certainly we are born with a temperament, and unless there is a chemical imbalance or illness, it can be directed into an attitude of gratitude.

It was 1992 and my husband had gone two full years without full-time employment. By now he had resorted to mowing lawns, cleaning out gutters, and cutting wood for people. Although trying so hard to be positive, I came to the breaking point. Our cars were in disrepair and we couldn't afford to fix them; we were one payment away from losing our home, and there was a whole day when we had absolutely no food to eat.

In the middle of the night I was crying on my pillow and so miserable that I came down to the music room and sat down at the piano. I always keep a legal pad and pencil handy in case I am inspired to write a song. Well, this night, I was not inspired. I was despondent. I sat at the keyboard grumbling and complaining between sobs.

Then a song began to run through my mind: "Count your blessings, name them one by one, Count your blessings see what God has done, Count your blessings, name them one by one, Count your many blessings, see what God has done."

Was there anything I could be thankful for in the midst of this terrible devastation? I took the pencil in hand and jotted down the first item on the legal pad:

Health. Yes, I was thankful that all of us were healthy. With no insurance, it would have been disastrous if one of us were ill.

Warmth. We have two wood burners and a friend allowed us access to his wood pile, so we would be warm all winter.

Clothing. Dear friends allowed us to wade through the bags of their "hand-me-over" clothes before sending them off to Goodwill. I never had worn name brands before!

Each other. No amount of money or material possessions could replace the love we have for each other as a family.

I filled up every line on two pages of legal pad! Then I turned to the Scripture that talked about how when Peter was in jail his friends prayed for him, and while they were praying, an angel appeared and set him free. I realized that the prayers of my friends had set me free from being enslaved to a bad attitude. The words and music just poured through my mind and spirit, and not long after that the song "Power When People Pray" became a reality. Listing my blessings in the middle of the darkest hour was a turning point for me. Even though we would suffer through another two years of financial devastation, choosing an attitude of gratitude gave us victory when to the world we looked like failures.

If you must worry, plan a time during the day and allow yourself to worry only during that time. This sounds a little strange, I admit, but this technique was the turning point in the life of one young woman. A college coed in the second semester of her sophomore year seemed to be doing just great. She was carrying a 3.5 GPA as she entered the semester, had a wonderful circle of Christian friends, and seemed to be blossoming while setting and attaining life goals.

Throughout the semester on visits home and calls back to her parents, everything seemed to be going beautifully. Then toward the end of the term, the parents received a call from the dean of students requesting a meeting. A meeting place between the two cities was agreed upon and the dean, the daughter, and the dad met.

As soon as the dad sat down at the table, the daughter immediately began sobbing. What on earth could the matter be? The dean had to coach her three times before she could blurt out, "I flunked every class this semester!"

How could a smart, well-adjusted girl with a history of academic and social success fail this miserably? Well, come to find out, she had fallen into a deep depression caused by low self-esteem. Because of this, she began skipping classes and falling behind on her work. There were stretches of three to four days when she wouldn't even leave her dorm room for meals, classes, or social gatherings.

Dad, of course, just hugged her and told her that they'd get through it. They moved her home and made an appointment to see a Christian psychologist. The first few meetings consisted of evaluation tests to determine the core problem. She was diagnosed with an anxiety syndrome. It seems that if there wasn't something valid to worry about, she'd create a disastrous scenario in her mind and worry about that.

Her whole day was filled with worry. The psychologist compared the energy she was expending with an air-conditioned room on a 100-degree day. With all of the doors and windows open, the air conditioner would expend all of its energy and never accomplish the cooling process. She, too, was expending all of her energies on worry so that there was no energy left to devote to school or relationships.

To help eliminate time spent on worry, the psychologist told her that she could worry only twice a day for a half hour each time. This meant that if a worry hit her at 8:30 A.M., she would have to wait until her assigned "worry time" at 10:30 A.M. to think about it again.

Believe it or not, she was able to see that she could control what she worried about and for how long. In fact, once 10:30 rolled around, she usually had forgotten what she was supposed to be worrying about.

I'm happy to report that this coed returned to school the next semester and earned a 4.0 GPA. She has learned to place her worry in the hands of God when things seem overwhelming. That young woman is our daughter, and we are so very proud of the courage and persistence she has displayed.

Control Your Responses

There are several creative ways to do this. One is the countdown method. Yes, grandmother knew best when she told you to count to ten before you reacted. You may need to begin at one hundred and count backwards.

Try body scanning. Begin at the top of your head and take an inventory throughout your body of where your most tense muscles are. Then tense and relax those muscles, holding the strain for about five seconds.

Many people find imagery helpful. Take a moment to lie down in the middle of a stressful situation. Imagine yourself in a beautiful outdoor setting by a babbling brook, colorful flowers, and a blue sky. Listen to soft music, "white" noise, or recorded outdoor sounds to divert your attention from the present tense.

Positive self-talk is another excellent way to gain control. "I feel bad that I didn't get the promotion, but there will be another opportunity. I feel good that I've been able to get to where I am." Or, "I'm very hurt the way my neighbor treated me, but I can't control her attitude toward me, only my attitude toward her."

Meditation and Prayer

Nothing takes the place of finding a quiet moment to, as the old hymn says, "Take it to the Lord in prayer!"

Be Realistic

Be certain to set realistic goals and expectations (of yourself and others). List your life achievement goals and ponder them. Prioritize them by assigning them a number. Under each goal, list the steps necessary for achievement, or begin a plan. Calculate the amount of time and the costs involved. Translate your goal into a daily calendar, allowing for the unexpected and proceed.

We set ourselves up for feeling like failures if we aren't realistic. My husband is a prime example. I took a look at his daily planner the other day to discover that there was absolutely no way he could possibly keep all the appointments he had made. His 9 A.M. meeting was followed by a 10 A.M. meeting. I asked how long his first meeting would probably take, and he thought about an hour. His next appointment was at least a fifteen-minute drive from his office. So, he would either leave one meeting early or get to the next one late.

When I looked at the tasks he was hoping to accomplish that day, I laughed. He would have only two hours in the office because of all his meetings, yet he had about ten hours worth of work he wanted to get done. "Are you planning on staying here all night?" I asked, the question loaded with meaning and carried with a smile. "Give me my planner back," he teased. "You act like you teach time management or something!" We laughed, but he got the point.

Control Your Schedule

Don't let your schedule control you. Keep a day planner of your choice. In it, include professional and personal appointments and keep it with you at all times. Pencil in appointments with yourself to avoid overcommitment. Here's the best advice few people ever take: Learn when to say *no*.

During stress management training with a group of pastors, I felt led to scold them a bit. I asked: "How many of you put pressure on the mother of a three year old to teach the three year olds' Sunday School class? Many sheepishly looked around at each other. I knew I had hit a nerve. "Shame on you!" I pointed my finger. "Quit asking her to do something unreasonable and then try to make her feel guilty if she says no!"

Likewise, when we are asked to add something to an already hectic schedule, reserve the right to handle it like this: "If you need an answer right now, it must be no, but if you want to give me a week to pray about it, check my schedule, and discuss it with my family, you may ask me about it next week."

I've learned that, yes, there are many things I can do, and I try to do them very well. But I can't do them all at the same time and still do them well while keeping balance in my life. There may be a season that a woman will want to teach three year olds, but it may be when her children are grown and she's got the time and patience to deal with this responsibility.

Advance Planning

Plan far in advance so that incidentals don't take time away from the important things. Being prepared for something is the best way to avoid being stressed about it later. Let's take Christmas, for example. It's on the same day each year, we are forewarned about its arrival through church, media, and small whiny children, yet many of us (me included!) put off the major portion of our shopping until the week of Christmas. Top this off with meal preparations for family get-togethers and we can hardly wait until the misery is over.

The most enjoyable holidays I've experienced are the ones when I've actually put on my day planner what things I should cook when before the holiday, and when I plan to shop for the ingredients. I invite guests into an organized and relaxed atmosphere where I'm not sidetracked by preparation (since it's already done) so I can focus on the most important thing: worshiping the Lord with friends and family.

Be Aware of Time Wasters

Can you name the top three? They are television, the telephone, and unnecessary meetings. Some experts tell us that the average American spends around four hours per day watching television. Unless the information we view is incredibly helpful, we are committed to a mindless activity for the equivalent of half a working day. I really didn't think I watched much television, but was shocked when during one winter, I crocheted ten sweaters to give as Christmas gifts. All of the work was done as I sat down to relax in front of the television after work. That was a wake-up call for me to put something more valuable in my mind and spirit than a senseless sitcom.

Care for Your Body

Exercise. Schedule your exercise time. Remember that it takes fifty calories to sustain the amount of muscle that fifteen calories sustain of fat. Only twenty minutes three times a week makes a big difference.

The other day my college-age son said, "Mom, I'm so tired all the time." It occurred to me that this former high school cross-country star and baseball player was so busy with classes and work that he wasn't doing anything physical. A week after pointing this out to him, he called home and said that he had begun rollerblading and couldn't believe all the energy he now had. Exercise is one of those life mysteries that doesn't seem to make any sense. Doesn't it seem that if we spend energy on physical activity that we will be tired and depleted of energy? Not so. The more energy we spend the more we earn.

Eat to stay healthy, not pencil thin. Yes, I've tried the no-fat diet, the no-carbohydrates diet, the cabbage soup diet, and so on. You have too, haven't you? Well, perhaps you found, like me, that it's better to exert some self-control on the intake amount and maintain a balance of nutritional foods. If you struggle with eating too much, I would suggest using your day planner to pencil in your mealtimes and what your menu needs to be so that you aren't caught off guard at the end of the day "starving" and wanting to eat everything in sight. Planning ahead and making a commitment to stick with the plan will help you stay healthy and keep those pounds off.

Indulge in a massage. Bob Hope (now in his 90s) receives a full body massage every day to keep joints limber, blood supply active, and to encourage the creation of new cells. Good circulation helps reduce high blood pressure and certainly relaxes the body.

Enjoy body oils and lotions. Psychologist Mary Hyink reminds us that stress in the form of loss or grief is expressed by the body through the skin. Therefore, soothing oils and lotions help to comfort a person in a stressful situation. Aroma therapy with scented candles has also proven to contribute to stress reduction.

Plan your sleep and rest times. The good news is that when we are deprived of sleep for a few nights, our bodies make up that loss in a couple of nights by not sleeping longer, but sleeping deeper, according to Dr. Mark Rosekind, an expert on sleep issues.[2] The bad news is that undersleeping by just two hours can hinder our ability to concentrate, solve problems, and think creatively.

Listen to your body. First Corinthians 6:19-20 reminds us of the awesomeness of the human body. "Do you not know that your body is a temple of the Holy Spirit, who is in you, whom you have received from God? You are not your own; you were bought at a price. Therefore honor God with your body."

It is no mistake that the analogy is made between our bodies and the temple of God. If we take a quick historical tour of Exodus 40:34 and 1 Kings 8:10-14, we find the record of the completion of the building of the tabernacle by Moses and the temple by Solomon.

Each worship center contained three main areas: the outer courtyard, that everyone could see and visit; the inner court, where select priests were allowed to enter; and finally, the Most Holy Place at the center. At the completion and dedication of both the tabernacle and the temple (with around four hundred years between the events), a cloud fills the Holy Place with the glory of the Lord. This is His dwelling place.

Our "temples" also represent three layers: the outer self that is visible to all, the inner self that a few intimates are allowed to see, and the innermost, which is our soul where the Most High yearns to sit on the throne. Because God dwells within us, we have an obligation to be cleansed from the inside out to make ourselves a worthy vessel for His use. Our spirits may be in perfect harmony with God, but we cannot be as effective in our ministry if our temple is not in top-performance condition.

A college classmate of my husband was an incredibly gifted songwriter who was saturated with a passion. He lived, breathed, and spoke music. Shortly after their graduation, we were saddened to hear that he had suddenly passed away. He was only in his twenties! Word got out that he was so obsessed with this God-given talent that he failed to take care of his body. He would go for a week without sleeping, pounding out music mercilessly on the piano. He refused to eat for long periods of time or exercise. So focused was he on this one dimension of his life that everything was out of balance. Because he did not listen to his body and treat it as the miraculous dwelling place of the Most High, neglect led to an early demise.

While we don't want to be self-absorbed or try to look like the models on TV and in magazines, we do want to make decisions that will lead to prolonged life and a high quality of life. We have a job to do in serving Christ, and we can't do that if our lives are cut short through our own neglect or abuse.

Use Color to Destress

Years ago my high school teaching load included the drama class. As a director, I consumed every book I could find on acting and producing so that we would offer the finest presentations. It quickly became apparent that the color of lighting and costumes would affect the emotions and reaction of the audience. So we dressed a king figure in purple, used red lighting for the fight scene, and soft blues for the transitions.

Confirming that color does in fact impact our stress level, one of my students brought in a newspaper article covering the stress level experienced at a maximum security prison. When the reporter asked how the prison dealt with violent criminals who were out of control, the guard said, "Let me take you to the holding area." He ushered the reporter into a room with no furniture, but the walls, ceiling, and floor were all painted a soft pink. "We just stick 'em in here for a few minutes and the pink room calms them right down!"

An oil company my husband worked for was owned by two brothers, the younger one passionate for the color red. As they chose colors to decorate their offices, he, of course, chose red. The carpeting was gray, the ceiling white, but all four walls were papered in a very bold red-and-gray design. Not long after moving into the newly decorated office, the brother began having headaches, was more irritable than usual, and found it hard to stay on task and concentrate for long periods of time. When he mentioned this to the interior designer, he said, "I'm not surprised! You've surrounded yourself with an angry color!"

Shortly after, they left the wall behind the desk papered in the bold red and changed the other three walls to gray. No more headaches, short temper, or lack of concentration.

Obviously the color of our rooms isn't going to totally take away our stress, but it can impact our emotions and contribute to destressing in a subtle way.

- Red makes us feel anger, passion, and hatred

- Blue makes us feel melancholy and quiet

- Green makes us feel young, energetic, and rejuvenated

- Yellow makes us feel cheery and warm

- Pink makes us feel relaxed[3]

How Did Jesus Handle Stress?

All stress isn't bad. In fact, the nervousness we feel making a presentation or running a race provides us with the energy and adrenaline to get the job done to the best of our ability. It's *what* we do with the stresses that we *are* going to face that determines our spiritual, emotional, and physical well-being.

Jesus exemplified a lifestyle that successfully dealt with stress—even the death on the cross. Look at some of the things He did that we can do to combat the stressors in our lives:

He Prayed

Many times the Bible records that Jesus removed Himself from the crowds and pressure and prayed. We even are allowed a glimpse into His adolescent worship habit. Luke 2:41-50 records the story of this twelve-year-old Jesus making the yearly Passover trek with His family and extended family to Jerusalem. Now put yourself in Mary's place and see if you wouldn't just feel like the most irresponsible mom. The Passover feast is done, so everyone in Jesus' family heads back to Nazareth.

After a day's journey home, they discover that Jesus was not—as they had supposed—with other relatives. Mary probably thought, "Oh, no! I've misplaced God!" So they traveled back to Jerusalem looking for Him. It was three days after returning to Jerusalem when they finally found Him. And where? "Why were you searching for me? . . . Didn't you know I had to be in my Father's house?" He had been in the temple "sitting among the teachers . . . and asking questions."

References are numerous to Jesus praying. We see Him praying during special occasions and turning points such as when He was baptized: "And as he was praying, heaven was opened and the Holy Spirit descended on him in bodily form like a dove" (Luke 3:21).

Luke 6:12 records Jesus in prayer before the choosing of the twelve disciples: "One of those days Jesus went out to a mountainside to pray, and spent the night praying to God."

Of course, the most poignant image we have of Jesus praying is in the Garden of Gethsemane where "being in anguish, he prayed more earnestly, and his sweat was like drops of blood falling to the ground" (Luke 22:44).

Scripture tells us, as in Luke 5:16, "Jesus often withdrew to lonely places and prayed." Praying alone for long periods of time marked Jesus' lifestyle and gave Him strength and wisdom to deal with the stress He faced. "After he had dismissed them, he went up on a mountainside by himself to pray. When evening came, he was there alone." (Matt. 14:23):

He Knew When to Say No

Matthew 14:13-21 records the miracle of the feeding of the five thousand (and this was just the number of men. There were women and children present as well). Jesus had just received word from His disciples that His cousin John the Baptist, who had baptized Him and proclaimed Him to all the world, had been beheaded by Herod.

Jesus "withdrew by boat privately," obviously to grieve His loved one's passing, yet the crowds found Him. He had compassion on them and healed their sick. They were hungry, and He fed them. But while they were still pressing in upon Him wanting to hear His teaching, wanting to be healed, needing His touch, He dismissed the crowd and went to a solitary place to pray.

Sometimes we feel that we are indispensable and don't have the right to say that our strength for that day is gone and we need some time to ourselves. Look to Jesus and know that there are times when we must say no.

Related to that, He recognized that He was not on earth to solve all of the world's problems. Matthew 26:11: "The poor you will always have with you." John 16:33: "In this world you will have trouble."

Our hope rests in the fact that *when* we face trials, we will receive encouragement from "the God of all comfort, who comforts us in all our troubles" (2 Cor. 1:3-4). When we rely on God in the middle of the stress, it allows us to "not rely on ourselves but on God. . . . He will deliver us" (2 Cor. 1:9-10). Not being able to solve all the world's problems is a good thing because it forces us to lean totally on God.

He Needed Rest and Solitude

Mark 6:31 tells us with so many people "coming and going," the disciples didn't even have a chance to eat. So Jesus kindly acknowledges this and says, "Come with me by yourselves to a quiet place and get some rest."

Of course, physical rest isn't the only rest that we need. Jesus invites us to "Come to me, all you who are weary and burdened, and I will give you rest" (Matt. 11:28). When we commit to spending time alone with Christ, He gives us both physical and emotional rest.

He Knew How to Delegate

After choosing and training the Twelve, Mark 6:7 tells us that He sent them out "two by two." He even "gave them power and authority to drive out all demons and to cure diseases" (Luke 9:1).

Later, we read that Jesus "appointed seventy-two others and sent them two by two ahead of him to every town and place where he was about to go" (Luke 10:1). Jesus, being God, could have done it all, yet He chose to bless those in His ministry by allowing them to grow from the power vested within them on His behalf.

Sometimes we think that by asking others to help us in our responsibility we are placing a burden on them, when in fact, when we delegate to them, we allow them to use their spiritual gifts and be pleasing to God.

He also depended upon a small inner core of followers. Many times John is referred to as the "beloved" disciple. We get a sense for the depth of Jesus' friendship and reliance upon John as we stand with him at the foot of the cross. Other disciples were notably absent, but John was there. "When Jesus saw his mother there, and the disciple whom he loved standing nearby, he said to his mother, 'Dear woman, here is your son' [referring to John], and to the disciple, 'Here is your mother.' From that time on, this disciple took her into his home" (John 19:26). So deep was the trust and respect that Jesus had for John that He assigned the earthly care of His mother into his hands.

In the Garden of Gethsemane, Jesus requested the presence of His inner core: Peter, James, and John. Although they fell asleep and just didn't quite "get it" as to what was about to happen, nonetheless, these are the friends Jesus chose to share His final hours with (Mark 14:32-34).

Apparently a special friendship had formed between Jesus and Mary Magdalene after He cast a demon out of her and she became a faithful follower. (See Luke 8:2.) Her presence is noted at the cross, burial, and resurrection. Likewise, we spread our burdens beyond our own shoulders when we can depend upon a few trusted friends to support us and be there for us in stressful times.

He Was Calm in the Midst of the Storm

Mark 4:38 reveals to us that "Jesus was in the stern, sleeping on a cushion" when the storm hit. I've often been amazed at how exhausted He must have been to be able to sleep through a dangerous storm that the Bible characterized as swamping the boat and putting them in great danger. Luke 8:24 says He "got up and rebuked the wind and the raging waters; the storm subsided, and all was calm."

When we face raging waters of stress that threaten to swamp us, if we call upon Him as the disciples did, the storm will subside and all will be calm. Even if our situation does not change, we can have an inner peace that only Christ can place in our hearts.

He Demonstrated Flexibility

Picture Jesus and His mom attending a wedding. The host runs out of wine, which would certainly be embarrassing to say the least. Jesus' mom, knowing full well His powers, and wanting to help her host save face, did what any other mom would do—she takes Him aside and says, "They have no more wine" (John 2:3). And Jesus gave the typical son reply, "Dear woman, why do you involve me? . . . My time has not yet come" (v.4).

Well, whether or not He thought His time to begin ministry had begun or not, Mom must have given the "mom look" that so many of us give to a son who is not being cooperative. She didn't even wait for Him to argue again, but told the servants, "Do whatever He tells you."

And as you know, He asked the servants to fill the large jars with water and draw some out for their master. The Bible says that it wasn't just turned into wine, but "the best wine."

It didn't seem that Jesus had planned on performing this miracle so He displayed a flexibility in doing so. Being flexible requires giving up some of our control and allowing others to participate in sharing our problem. In this case, Jesus' first recorded miracle officially began His ministry and the miracle "revealed his glory, and his disciples put their faith in him." Mom knew best!

He Was Submissive

The word submissive isn't real popular in today's culture. We get the picture of a browbeaten husband, a doormat wife, or Ms. Milquetoast at work.

When Jesus prayed to the Father "take this cup from me" (referring to the separation from the Father He would experience while on cross), He submitted Himself to God the Father by saying, "Yet not my will, but yours be done" (Luke 22:42). Has there ever been a more pure example of servant leadership in all of history?

Giving up what we feel are our rights is one of the most difficult things to do. Yet sometimes it's that fighting to hang onto something and do it "*my way*" that causes great and unnecessary stress in our lives.

Each major and routine activity recorded about Jesus reveals that He was totally submitted to the will of His Father in heaven. Think of it: He gave up a kingly crown and heavenly glory to be humbled as a helpless human baby who could not walk, talk, or care for Himself. It would seem that we too should submit our walk, talk, and care humbly to God the Father.

He Had Compassion

He allowed compassion to divert Him from His original plan. In keeping with being totally submitted and surrendered to what His purpose was, Mark 6:34 tells us "When Jesus landed and saw a large crowd, he had compassion on them, because they were like sheep without a shepherd. So he began teaching them many things." Matthew 14:14: "He had compassion on them and healed their sick."

Jesus, the master storyteller, encourages us to allow compassion to take priority over controlling our own plan. In Luke 10 He tells the now familiar story of a man beaten and robbed by thieves and left in the ditch for dead. Two men who did not allow compassion to divert them from getting to their destination as planned passed by the helpless victim. However, the Good Samaritan "took pity on him," bandaged his wounds, and put the man on his own donkey to get him to a place of safety and rest.

Think of the blessings we miss by sticking too strictly to our own plans. May we look with the same eyes of compassion on a wounded world as did Jesus and allow His plans to be our priority. When we do His will, stress melts away.

Don't Worry; Be Happy!

Years ago when this seemingly airhead song hit the pop charts with a Caribbean rhythm, I thought, "How irresponsible!" However, as I've studied more and more the teachings of Christ, this is exactly the message that He gives to you and me. He doesn't want us to be stressed or worried about anything. In fact He tried to minimize our stresses and put them into perspective. Consider the following passages:

"Who of you by worrying can add a single hour to his life? Since you cannot do this *very little thing*, why do you worry about the rest?" (Luke 12:25-26, italics added).

Jesus refers to adding hours to our life as a little thing. For centuries, man has searched for the fountain of youth and has tried to find a way to be immortal. It's a human impossibility, yet for God it is "a very little thing"! If what seems so impossible to us is a very little thing in God's economy, it should tell us right there that worrying isn't going to profit us anything, so why waste the time?

"Come to me, all you who are weary and burdened, and I will give you rest. Take my yoke upon you and learn from me, for I am gentle and humble in heart, and you will find rest for your souls. For my yoke is easy and my burden is light" (Matt. 11:28-30).

Rest for our souls. It's one thing to endure physical exhaustion, but what a beautiful promise of giving us a rest from our spiritual burden.

A farmer once explained to me that when oxen were used to till the soil, the yoke had two neck openings so that a pair of oxen could pull the plow together. When a young ox was old enough to begin the training process, he would be yoked with an older, more experienced, ox. Since the younger ox didn't yet have the physical strength to carry the weight of the plow, the older ox actually performed all of the work, carrying the entire weight while the younger simply walked in step beside.

So it is when we take up Christ's yoke. He walks beside us carrying the burden so that our load is light.

"Cast all your anxiety on him because he cares for you" (1 Peter 5:7). "Cast your cares on the Lord and He will sustain you" (Ps. 55:22.)

When I was about ten, my dad took me fishing for the first and last time. He baited the hook, helped me reel in the fish, then took the fish off the hook. But I had lots of fun being with him and watching him fish for me.

When I think of casting my anxiety on Christ, I think of casting that fishing line. If I can attach my burden to the end of that line and cast it into the deep, cleansing waters, it only remains my anxiety if I choose to reel it back in again. Christ wants us to give Him the worries and let Him keep them.

"Do not be anxious about anything, but in everything, by prayer and petition, with thanksgiving, present your requests to God" (Phil. 4:6).

I have a three-step process I use to destress: I pray, I make a request, and I give thanks. And I've found that God is always faithful.

Submission Test

Remember that day I told you about when I sat at the keyboard counting my blessings and writing "Power When People Pray?" Earlier that day I had donned my running shoes, grabbed the leash for the German shepherd, and darted out the drive.

I began praying, well, grumbling, to God. The madder I got the faster I ran! Finally, in my mind I yelled at God saying, "Look, when are we going to get our life back? I just want to be normal again. If You're trying to teach me something, then hit me over the head with it so I understand!"

I didn't finish a half a step when so clearly in my spirit God said, "Julie, I've allowed this situation to take place as an answer to your prayers."

"Huh? I can't say as if I remember asking for You to take away all of our material possessions and not provide for our children!"

"I'm answering every prayer you've ever had for your children and I'm doing it through your financial devastation."

"Whoa! What?"

Then God put me through a little quiz. I encourage you to take it too. As I answered these three questions, it clarified for me who I am in relation to who God is:

1. Do you believe God is sovereign?

2. Do you believe God has a plan for your life?

3. Are you willing to submit to that plan?

Numbers one and two were easy for me to answer yes to, but I really struggled with number three.

Do You Believe God Is Sovereign?

The definition of sovereign is "possessed of supreme power; ruler, unlimited in extent; absolute."

"Acknowledge that the Most High is sovereign over the kingdoms of men" (Dan. 4:25).

"Great is our Lord and mighty in power" (Ps. 147:5).

"God, the blessed and only Ruler, King of kings and Lord of lords, who alone is immortal and who lives in unapproachable light" (1 Tim. 6:15).

Do You Believe God Has a Plan for Your Life?

"But the plans of the Lord stand firm forever, the purposes of his heart through all generations" (Ps. 33:11).

"Many are the plans in a man's heart, but it is the Lord's purpose that prevails" (Prov. 19:21).

"A man's steps are directed by the Lord. How then can anyone understand his own way?" (Prov. 20:24).

Can You Submit to God's Plan for Your Life?

"How much more should we submit to the Father of our spirits and live!" (Heb. 12:9).

"Submit yourselves, then, to God. Resist the devil, and he will flee from you" (James 4:7).

"Humble yourselves before the Lord, and he will lift you up" (James 4:10).

God *is* sovereign and He *does* have a plan for our lives. If we submit to that plan, no matter what the cost or the hardship, we have learned the first and most important lesson in stress management.

Perhaps we can easily summarize these ideas by remembering them as the three A's to destressing:

Analyze what is in your sphere of influence.

Admit what can and cannot be changed.

Accept and submit to God's plan.

Submitting is a daily giving over, yet surrender does not prove us powerless but powerful.

Here's another acronym for STRESS that may give you encouragement when anxiety begins working its way into your life:

Seek Him

Trust Him

Rest in Him

Enjoy Him

Submit to Him

Sit with Him

I don't know what kind of stress you are facing today, but I know that unless you are room temperature and not breathing, you have stress! If you have just been uprooted or faced a loss, I pray that God will graciously surround you with loving relationships that will fill that void.

If you are facing financial struggles, remember that "my God will meet all your needs according to his glorious riches in Christ Jesus" (Phil. 4:19).

If you are facing unresolved relational issues, take heart that Jesus gave His all for you, proving His friendship and love. He is all we need. He was willing to lay down his life for a friend (John 15:13). He will never leave you nor forsake you (Heb. 13:5).

If you are facing tragic circumstances out of your control or wish that you could control the attitudes and behavior of another human being, surrender your anxiety to the Lord and ask friends to uplift you in prayer.

Finally, if like so many of us, you feel that you have too much to do and not enough time to do it, read on! Our next chapter is going to deal with specific ways that you can manage your time so that you are fulfilling God's purposes in your life and not getting sidetracked or committed to the nonessentials.

Then, whenever you feel that stress is taking over, return to this exercise and practice this relaxation technique. I often have wondered if this were the type of thing Jesus practiced as He prepared for prayer alone with His Father:

- Sit in a chair (with arms) and close your eyes

- Rest your arms and let them completely relax

- Breathe deeply from the abdomen

- Scan for muscle tension

- Tense specific muscle groups for five seconds, then release/relax

- Visualize the muscles relaxing

- Imagine warmth filling each muscle

- Repeat again on extremely tense areas starting from head to toe

- Breathe deeply from the abdomen

- Open your eyes and feel refreshed!

Father, we commit to You all of our anxiety, worry, and stress.
We commit and submit it to You and acknowledge Your sovereignty.
Allow us to take up Your yoke so that we can walk beside You,
letting You carry our burden. Amen.

If I Only Had Thirty-Four Hours in a Day, Everything Would Be All Right
Time Management

We are always complaining that our days are few, and acting as if there would be no end to them. Let's make haste to live since every day to a wise man is a new life.

—Seneca

C onsider the following which so dramatically captures the essence of time and its value.

Imagine there was a bank which credits your account each morning with $86,400, carries no balance from day to day, allows you to keep no cash balance, and every evening cancels whatever part of the amount you had failed to use during the day. What would you do? Draw out every cent, of course!

Well, everyone has such a bank. Its name is *time*. Every morning, it credits you with 86,400 seconds. Every night it writes off, as lost, whatever of this you have failed to invest to good purpose. It carries no balance. It allows no overdraft. Each day it opens a new account for you. Each night it burns the records of the day. If you fail to use the day's deposits, the loss is yours. There is no going back. There is no drawing against tomorrow.

We must live in the present on today's deposits. Invest so as to get from it the utmost in health, happiness, and success. The clock is running. Make the most of today.

Take a moment to ponder these things:

To realize the value of ONE YEAR: Ask the student who has failed her final exam.

To realize the value of ONE MONTH: Ask the mother who has given birth to a premature baby.

To realize the value of ONE WEEK: Ask the editor of a weekly newspaper.

To realize the value of ONE DAY: Ask a daily wage laborer who has ten kids to feed.

To realize the value of ONE HOUR: Ask the lovers who are waiting to meet.

To realize the value of ONE MINUTE: Ask a person who has missed the train.

To realize the value of ONE SECOND: Ask the person who survived an accident.

To realize the value of ONE MILLISECOND: Ask the person who won the silver medal in the Olympics.

To realize the value of ONE LIFETIME: Ask someone who missed his chance.

Treasure every moment that you have. And treasure it more because you shared it with someone special. . . . Special enough to have your time. And remember—time waits for no one. . . . We make a living by what we get, but we make a life by what we give."[1]

The Proverbs 31 Woman

I don't know about you, but whenever anyone begins to quote this chapter, I begin to slouch in my chair and look at the floor. What an impossible standard to live up to, we say. Yet, this composite portrait displays to us the very essence of how we women should make time for our highest priorities.

She is first praised because of her character. As we read on we discover that she brings good to her husband and provides a role model in her household that exemplifies hard work, taking responsibility, and even running a business. She has compassion on the poor and keeps her sense of humor. She can speak with wisdom and give instruction to her family because of her reliance upon the Lord.

Her circumstances, though in a different setting and age, are very similar to ours. She, too, was trying to juggle a variety of responsibilities so that her ripple effect extended out to her family and community. As we discuss practical ways to save and manage our time, let us be ever mindful of keeping these same priorities and weighing the worth of every activity against them.

"Guard well your spare moments. They are like uncut diamonds. Discard them and their value will never be known; improve them and they will become the brightest gems in useful life."[2]

The Juggler

Consider the artful juggler and you understand the act almost every woman is trying to perfect. Something is always in the air threatening to crash down around her feet. She can't hold onto everything at one time; it's an endless cycle. She feels she's caught in an eternal tornado with time sweeping her off her feet and spinning her out of control.

We say that spending time with our kids is our priority, but there's laundry to do and meals to prepare. We know that we need to exercise, but there is cleaning to do, work in the briefcase from the office, and we're too tired. We intend to read our Bible and pray, but, well, that *People* magazine looked too enticing.

The truth of an old essay often rings in my ears when I think about how time gets the better of us—*The Tyranny of the Urgent*. The point is that we need to be aware of what is truly important to us—and live our lives doing what is important to us. If we don't, we will likely spend the majority of our time putting out fires and dealing with emergencies. Who wants to live like that? Probably no one, yet many of us do.

We look at our commitments, responsibilities, and dreams, and it seems as if we're standing at the base of Mt. Everest wondering how we can possibly ever conquer the mountain.

Well, as the old saying goes, what's the best way to eat an elephant? Answer: one bite at a time! We must learn to break the big jobs down into smaller, more palatable jobs—and this, only after determining whether the task underscores our value system and priorities. An old Chinese proverb states that "The journey of a thousand miles begins with a single step." It may look like a long road ahead, so let's take a few of those steps together on the journey of mastering time so that time doesn't master us.

Which Woman Am I Right Now?

Remember that song I referred to a few chapters back that validated unrealistic expectations of women? It went like this: "I can bring home the bacon, fry it up in the pan, and never ever let you forget you're a man . . . I'm a woman . . . W-O-M-A-N . . . Let me sing it again."

How many of us have bought into this myth that we should feel guilty if we can't work a full-time job, perfect the tasks of the full-time homemaker, and still have enough left over to give full attention to our man (and kids) at the end of the day? We're trapped in several worlds and asking ourselves, Which woman am I right now? Am I the suave professional working woman diligently tackling her job responsibilities, or am I the Susie homemaker attempting to decorate my house and cook like Martha Stewart? Or am I the PTA leader, good neighbor, and Bible study teacher? Can these worlds ever connect without colliding?

Time management involves managing *all* of our time for all of our worlds, so we must have a plan of action that successfully meshes the professional with the personal. That familiar passage from Ecclesiastes 3:1 begins: "There is a time for everything, and a season for every activity under heaven." Are we spending time doing the right thing—but in the wrong season of our lives? Are we guilty of the tyranny of the urgent? Do our activities underscore the things that are most important to us?

Because one person cannot live in multiple worlds, we've got to merge all of our activities and responsibilities into one time management system. This means that we must allow time for all aspects of who we are and who we are in the process of becoming.

Merging Professional with Personal

The best advice I can give to you is this: use a planning calendar that includes room for daily, monthly, yearly, and even multiyear planning. Only when you put it in writing will you remember appointments. Only when you put it in writing will you visualize a long-term goal. Only when you put it in writing can you see what's eating your day away. Here are the things that are absolutely necessary in a planner:

A yearly planner. Mark out vacation weeks, annual doctor's appointments, and personal days before the year ever gets started. This way you will save time for your personal rest and rejuvenation.

A month at a glance. Here you note all major upcoming events including meetings, appointments, trips, and important celebrations. These eventually get included on your daily appointment calendar, with more detail (such as phone numbers, directions, and costs).

A daily appointment calendar. This should not only include a timeline where daily appointments can be documented, but should allow for a listing of your goals and most important items to get done. It should also include space for taking notes from phone calls. Your notes become a legal document that stand up in court should there be confusion or a dispute.

An expense log where you can document mileage and other business expenses, as well as personal ones.

An address directory with space for phone and fax numbers.

A month-at-a-glance planning calendar that projects at least two years into the future.

Using a Time Management System

Include all personal and professional appointments and notes. This way you see possible crossover conflicts and don't overlook picking up dry cleaning after work or getting that letter in the mail.

Carry the calendar with you at all times. In fact, many experts suggest that you even lay it on your bedside stand during the night. This way, as an idea hits you, or an appointment is made, you can always make a note of it on the appropriate page. In addition, you always have your phone directory with you and won't be tempted to take notes on a sticky pad which will ultimately stick to the bottom of your shoe or the lining of your purse before you can get it into the house and write it down.

Ta-daa! Now your worlds can become merged without colliding!

Before we look at schedules and keeping track of appointments and commitments, let's get one thing straight. You can't do everything. Life is filled with making choices based on your value system. Philosopher William James once said, "The art of being wise is the art of knowing what to overlook." Too many priorities can paralyze us; wise women learn to say no to the good so they can say yes to the better.

With that in mind, what types of things are you going to allow to make their way onto your calendar? Before penciling in a certain commitment, ask yourself the three questions that leadership expert John Maxwell notes. He makes the point that the last thing we know is what to put first. Therefore assess the importance of an item by asking:

What is required of me? (*What is it that no one but me can do?*)

What gives me the greatest return? (*Am I doing what I do best and receiving a good return for the organization?)*

What is most rewarding? *(When something is a success,
it's not work; it's a way of life.)*[3]

It's okay to develop a system of "planned neglect." For instance, when our daughter was faced with a grueling semester of college classes and trying to work full time, she realized that there were certain things she wouldn't have time for in those months: cooking, socializing, thoroughly cleaning her apartment, and dealing with nitty-gritty details. She temporarily put some priority items on hold—short-term sacrifice for long-term gain.

I often tell my staff that there *will* be things that we need to let fall through the cracks. I wish all details could be tied up into a neat bow with a card attached, but reality dictates otherwise. One year we tried to help TimeOut for Women! conference attendees by allowing lunch reservations to be made from the arena during the morning break. It proved disastrous because the restaurants that signed women up didn't honor the reservations once they got to the restaurant. We looked bad and sacrificed the time of several volunteers to coordinate the effort.

Because of experiences like this, when we begin tossing around some very good ideas, I've learned to bring everyone back on course by asking one question: "Will this minister?" That's our priority. That's what our value system is based upon. If the item discussed has little impact on our effectiveness in reaching women for the Lord, we usually table the idea or bury it.

As one leadership expert stated, "Don't be afraid to bury a bad idea. The corpse doesn't smell any better the longer you keep it around."

So let's talk about some good ideas that do deserve to be adopted into a daily life regimen. First we'll take a look at some things you can do in your home to save time and stress, and then some things that will help you keep your sanity in your professional setting.

Personal Time Savers

Rescued from the Dirty Clothes Bag

When our kids were in elementary school, it was the biggest miracle to get them up on time, dressed in clothes that had not been rescued from the dirty clothes basket, placing in their hand a lunch sack containing something that resembled a sandwich, and off to the bus stop before the bus passed our drive. I used to close the door behind me and literally lean back on it sighing with closed eyes due to the stress of it all.

Then, many days I was either off to work or faced with the overwhelming task of looking at the results of our household hurricane asking, "Where do I begin?" Here is a routine that has worked well for me and alleviated tackling a mountain of laundry:

The night before:

- Make kids' lunches

- Prepare morning coffee by setting the coffee maker's timer

- Decide the next evening's menu and take things out to thaw

- Run the dishwasher

The morning of:

- Get myself ready and make sure kids are getting up

- Make our bed

- Collect all dirty laundry in the master bedroom and bath

- Stop into bedroom of child number 1 and help make bed, add laundry to my basket

- Stop into bedroom of child number 2 and help make bed, add laundry to my basket

- Add any towels or items lying around to the basket

- Put load of laundry in washer

- Empty dishwasher while coaxing the kids to eat breakfast

- Pray with kids, hug them, and shoo them out the door—hoping they'll eat that granola bar on the way

- Lean back against the door and thank God for another miracle

After work and school:

- Whoever is home first puts the laundry in the dryer

- After dinner, assign family member to fold the laundry and return to drawers and linen closets

Somehow, when the laundry is done, the dishes are clean, and the beds are made, we can breathe a little deeper feeling that things are somewhat under control.

For a creative person who hates routine, this has not been a fun or easy schedule for me to keep. However, one load of laundry per day means that I don't have seven loads on Saturday. It also gives opportunity to delegate simple chores to family members.

Love to Eat; Hate to Cook

What's the first question most kids ask when they bop in the door after school? You got it: "Mom, what's for dinner?" Dinner? Oops. How'd that slip my mind?

If you're like me, you may really love to cook, but not when you're dog tired after a hard day of working. Cooking can be hard work all by itself. We have to decide on a menu, shop for the ingredients, then somehow whip everything up so that it all comes out hot just at the time when the family is finally all home to eat it.

Here are some tips that can save you time in the kitchen:

Grocery shop just once per month at a bulk food store. If you shop at nonpeak hours, you will not have to wait for your turn in the soup aisle or at the cash register. Buying in bulk saves money too.

Cook a whole week's or a whole month's worth of meals and freeze. One of my favorite cookbooks for this was written by three of my dear Christian friends in Colorado and it's called *Don't Panic . . . It's in the Freezer*. If you can't find it at your local store, write to them at 410 S. Otis Street, Lakewood, CO 80226. Be sure to tell them that Julie Baker sent you. (I don't even get a kickback.)

Get out your monthly calendar and decide which day of the month and what time will work best for you to do the bulk shopping. If you have a child or husband who can lend you a hand, be sure to draft her or him. Then, choose a different day to actually cook in bulk. This way, after shopping for groceries, you can stop at the dollar store, enjoy a frozen yogurt, and window shop at the bargain boutique without feeling rushed to get home.

Choose to make entrees with like ingredients. For instance, brown several pounds of low-fat ground beef and use part of it for a sloppy Joe mix, part for spaghetti sauce, and part for chili. All of these recipes also call for onions, tomato sauce, and possibly green peppers, so you can have a family member help you cut vegetables that will work in all dishes.

Cook with a friend. My how the time flies when cutting up together—vegetables that is.

If Cleanliness Is Next to Godliness . . . I'm in Trouble.

A friend of mine maintains that cleaning is so relaxing to her that she just looks forward to it every Saturday. She should get therapy.

Most of us probably don't anticipate cleaning with great joy, and if you're like me, you still try to do your best to, as my grandma used to say, "keep things up." A few simple tips can save us cleaning time:

Place absorbent washable rugs in the entryway to your home. Much cleaning can be eliminated if dirt never has a chance to get past the front door.

Clean top to bottom, cleaner to dirtier. For instance, when cleaning your bathroom, use glass cleaner to shine the mirror first. Then, either using glass cleaner or a stronger all-purpose cleaner, wash off the countertop and scrub the sink. Wipe down the shower or tub, and finally, scour the toilet. Empty the paper basket and vacuum. Done. (Note: a sanitized bathroom is the best way to ward off spreading germs and colds. One mom raised six kids alone and cleaned the bathroom every morning after the kids left for school and before she went to work. The kids were hardly ever sick.)

Clean the kitchen as you cook. Don't give anything a chance to dry onto the pan, dish, or counter. At least rinse and place in the dishwasher or set in warm dishwater to soak.

Spray surfaces with all-purpose cleaner and let sit for three to five minutes before wiping up. This eliminates time-consuming and strenuous scrubbing.

If you really want to be organized, place cleaning tasks in your weekly calendar so that you know what you need to do and when. Perhaps a little cleaning everyday suits your personality and energy level. Or some prefer blocking out a few hours in one day when they get a majority of the cleaning taken care of. Seasonal items such as washing windows, cleaning curtains, or shampooing carpets can also be noted on your calendar. One thing is for sure—if most of us wait to do these things until we're in the mood, it will never get done.

Hire and delegate when possible. The very busy woman needs to concentrate on the things that only she can do and delegate other tasks as much as possible. If you fit into this category, don't feel guilty for getting help. It will be a blessing to you and free you up to accomplish the things that are unique to you.

Bill, Bill, Junk Mail, Bill, Oooh—Letter from Aunt Mary

Whether rain or shine . . . there is mail to open. Mail can be a blessing *and* a curse. With more mailing lists being sold from one company to the next, we are inundated with stuff we never asked to receive. It's like having a complete stranger walk up our sidewalk and knock on our door unannounced and unwelcome. How can we keep incoming mail from being a time waster?

It has been said that each piece of mail should be handled only once and should have one of four things happen to it:

- Do it

- Delegate it

- Delay it

- Dump it

Junk Mail

Obviously mail needs to first be sorted. I don't even open junk mail. It goes into file 13 the moment it hits the front door. The only exception to my rule is January, which has proved to be the highest month of readability for all mail. I guess it's Christmas card let down or something.

Bills

Bills cannot be delayed or delegated; they need our immediate attention. Some pay bills as soon as they receive them. Others create a "tickler" file where bills are placed in a folder for the day of the month they need to be sent. In either case, a plan is in place so that important commitments are not overlooked or forgotten. The bill needs to be handled only once before being paid.

Letters, Interesting Magazines, and Catalogs

If you're like me, you can hardly wait to open up a card or letter that is sent by a friend or relative. However, if time does not allow for you to read it or your favorite magazine or catalog when it arrives, create a reading file, tray, or basket so that you can return to relish your reading later in the day when you have a few moments.

Outgoing Mail

To save time and money, send out a postcard instead of a letter. It's cheaper and you don't have to search for an envelope.

Take advantage of a pick-up service for packages. Even the U.S. Postal Service now has an 800 number you can call to help you ship something out.

If you are computer savvy and have a database program, schedule some time to input the names and addresses of those to whom you want to send Christmas cards or family updates. The addresses can be printed out on labels so that when it comes time for mailing something to all of your friends, you just press "print" and *voila*! No looking up addresses and writing them out by hand. It also serves as a hand dandy reference when you can't find the address in your Rolodex or day planner directory.

I'm Sorry, the Doctor Just Left for an Emergency

Emergencies can conflict with an appointment you have scheduled any time of day, but here are some pointers for appointments:

Schedule routine dentist and doctor appointments during the least busy times of the year. January and June seem to be better times. Avoid combating the lines during the before-school sports-season craze.

Try to be the first patient in the morning. This way you won't have to wait for other appointments that have gone long and infringed upon your scheduled time.

Take your day planner to the appointment with you so that you can set up your next visit as you check out.

True, there are many incidentals and things about our personal routine with family that get out of control, but these timesaving tips may allow for keeping some sense of order amid the chaos.

Professional Time-Savers

Even though the following suggestions are streamlined for the women who also work outside the home in a professional position, many of these suggestions are helpful to those who are their home's number one administrator or whose outside jobs allow less control of their environment.

Can you believe that the average manager will encounter at least two hundred interruptions on the job each day? It's a wonder we get anything accomplished.

There are six roots to interruptions:

- Walk-ins

- The telephone

- Lack of planning

- Lack of prioritizing

- Lack of organization

- Lack of focus

Let's take a look at each root of interruption and then talk about some specific ways to put a stop to being stopped.

Walk-ins

Position your desk facing away from the door. Many work environments either have windows in the doors or cubicles with no doors, so it makes workers seem easily accessible. If you are facing toward that opening, it is easy to catch an eye or be distracted as someone walks by. Then it becomes almost impossible to avoid a lengthy exchange which eats up time. This is one case where it's okay to turn a cold shoulder so as to avoid an interruption.

Use your door as a signal. You can make it known that your door's position designates your availability. An open door signals that it's okay to approach. A half-open door means that you are on task, but may be able to handle an interruption. A closed door means that you are absolutely *not* available.

The Telephone

I've often called the telephone "the piece we hold to our heads that robs us of our time." It is both our friend and foe. It can be our greatest asset or our liability, depending upon how we control its use.

Incoming

Use caller ID. You can count on an "unavailable" or "out of area" call during the dinner hour being a solicitation call you don't want to take. On the other hand, you can see immediately if that return call you're waiting for is coming in so you can answer it immediately. Another advantage? A record of calls are kept so that you can check it later if you've misplaced a phone number.

Let voice mail take it. Many times phone calls are made to exchange information. This can effectively be left on voice mail. I love to talk and be friendly, but don't always have time to chat. Leaving a message alleviates taking time for the polite amenities—how are the kids, is hubby over the flu, where are you going on vacation. . . .

Have staff screen calls. Few of us have the luxury of having a staff member who can answer our phone and screen calls. If you do, use it and enjoy it. This way calls can be prioritized so that only the most important interrupt your day. In addition, the person answering may be able to solve the issue at hand so that you never are interrupted.

Keep calls short. The person calling you has called because it is a convenient time for him or her. It may not be the best time for you, so let the caller know it must be a short conversation. When talk begins to hop down a bunny path leading you to a different destination than the purpose of the call, wrap it up.

Use time cues. Here are some phrases that really get the point across: I was just on my way out. Someone is in my office. I'm on deadline. I have a meeting soon. I need to let you go.

Leave a detailed outgoing message on your voice mail. I try to answer the typical questions asked and give resource numbers to call during my outgoing message. Probably half of my calls end up being hang-ups who got their answer without our even having a conversation.

Outgoing

Plan a specific time to make and return phone calls. As you look at your appointment calendar, don't forget to budget time for this most important task. It is probable that you will catch only one out of every six people you try to reach, but try to budget enough time to get to all calls made. Perhaps you can let it be known that from 4 to 5 P.M. you will return calls, so colleagues can expect a call back then or know they can reach you during this time period.

Group together your return calls. Batching like tasks together saves time, so when returning one call, return several at the same time.

Outline your comments beforehand. Nothing wastes more time than finally reaching the person you need to talk to, then forgetting some of the points you want to cover. In your daily appointment calendar, list the important things you need to talk about before making the call. Then, as the conversation progresses, take notes next to each item so that you have a written record. An old Chinese proverb states that the palest ink outlasts the longest memory.

Set up a phone meeting. So much can be accomplished in a phone call and can spare us from attending a dreaded meeting. Find a time when all parties are available to discuss a particular issue, then pencil it in on the appointment calendar. Schedule time for it just as you would for a fifteen-minute or half-hour meeting.

Limit the time you spend per call. Whether responding to an incoming call, returning a call, or setting up a phone meeting, set time parameters for the call. "I have five minutes, then I'm off to another meeting." The other meeting may just be another telephone call you need to return. Say you have ten calls to return. If each lasts five minutes, you've burned up the better part of an hour—not to mention the work that may be generated from each call. At least by agreeing to a time limit on the call, both you and the person you're talking to know when it's time to move on to something else.

Send a memo, e-mail, or fax. Depending upon your keyboard ability, this may or may not be a time-saver. However, if information needs to be relayed for discussion later, a written document may not only save you phone time, but also allow there to be no confusion concerning the message.

Call early, call late. If you just need to receive or send an informational message, use voice mail. You are most likely to access voice mail before or after hours. Group ten return phone calls and make them after hours, and what might take fifty minutes in conversations could take only ten minutes of leaving messages.

And proper phone etiquette dictates that rather than just saying, "Please give me a call at . . . ," that you actually give an inkling as to what you want to talk about: "Sue, I'm looking for the memo we sent to Mr. Smith and wonder if you could fax me a copy."

When used effectively, the telephone can be a great asset. When we're inefficient, the telephone can rob us of valuable time and become a frustrating and irritating interruption in our day.

Learn to Plan

We will give more detailed information about planning and goal setting in another chapter, but here are some basic ways that forward planning can save time and alleviate stress:

Keep an appointment calendar. Use it as a way to stay on track with each day's activity and to assist you in forward planning on any long-term project or goal you want to attain.

Let your coworkers and family know your schedule. Nothing beats good communication between people when it comes to avoiding conflicts and double bookings.

Some new computer software packages are available that allow an entire office to access a general weekly office planner as well as the appointment calendar of each staff member. This way, when looking at a meeting time that is convenient for each staff member, one only needs to bring up each person's monthly schedule and find a date and time that is open for all, input the meeting information on each calendar as well as the general staff calendar, and the announcement is made. Think of the time this saves when compared to reaching each person individually and talking through a possible meeting time.

For example, you might specifically schedule time for:

- Phone calls

- Writing

- Creative thinking

- Meetings

- Bible reading and devotions

Communicate times you need privacy to work. If you've taken to heart the art of planning how you spend your time, you can convey to others when you are not available. It may mean that you actually take the laptop and retreat to another location for the duration of a project. This is not being rude; it's just good time management that allows you to fulfill your responsibility.

Learn to Prioritize

Again, are we spending time on things that are important to our value system, or are we running around, out of control, doing any tasks that hit our desk in just any order? If we learn to prioritize our tasks in the order of their importance, we can at least evaluate what deserves our attention and what may need to be tabled or even discarded.

List your goals. These goals may be just those things that are required of you on the job, or can also include personal goals. If you sit down once a week, possibly on the weekend, and just list the tasks that need to be accomplished for the following week, you begin the workweek with a sense of direction.

Prioritize your goals. After you've listed all of your goals, pray over them, think about the goals in terms of your job description, and then evaluate the strengths that you can offer to each item. Then, in the margin, simply begin designating the most important goal that needs accomplishing by putting a 1 next to it, a 2 next to the second most important task, and so on.

Translate these priority goals to your next week's or month's appointment calendar. If you need to brainstorm to begin a new project, pencil in an hour on Monday to "dream and scheme." Then, schedule another hour on Tuesday to create a project timeline for this item. Note any meetings that need to be scheduled and pencil in time on your appointment calendar to contact those who need invitations to the meeting.

Measure all deeds against the accomplishment of those goals. My husband, who has been a full-time fund-raiser for nonprofit organizations, always has his staff ask: "What difference will the task I'm performing right now make to our ultimate goal?" If it makes very little, he encourages the staff member to evaluate the worthiness of the task. However, if it is a building block toward the final goal, then it becomes a priority item.

Plan far enough in advance so that a routine task does not become an emergency item. Christmas falls on the same date each year, yet how many of us act as if it was a last-minute afterthought? As I mentioned before, I've been guilty of waiting until the week of Christmas to shop and it makes the whole week an unenjoyable whirlwind of exhausting activity. What should be a blessing becomes an unpleasant emergency. However, when I plan several short shopping excursions during the off-season, I enjoy it and enter the holiday season with my focus where it belongs—on Jesus Christ—not my shopping list.

Learn to Organize

Being neat is more than a neurotic compulsion. It can save us time. If you've ever watched a car mechanic, you have seen the value of organizing a work space. He places every tool on a rolling tray, and each wrench and whatchamacallit is placed in the very same place on the tray. He doesn't even have to look, but can just reach for the right tool when he needs it.

We can also benefit from a sense of order in our offices and homes.

Organize your work space. Place the items that you use most in closest proximity. I've even begun placing the address cards that I access the most often in the front of my Rolodex. I file them under the first letter of the last name or company, but within that letter, I place the cards I use most at the front for quick access. I try also to discard anything as it becomes obsolete.

Create a file for all documents. It's amazing how fuzzy our minds feel when all the papers we need to do something about are sitting on our desk piled on top of each other. However, if we take a little time to think through and create a filing system, each item that comes across our desk can have a special home. You may even want to create files close by for reading, invoices, projects, and "gotta get done today." If you suffer from out of sight, out of mind, keep a stackable file on your desk so that looking at the files reminds you to deal with them.

Modify and create as you go along. Be sure to change or add space or file topics as your projects expand and evolve. Change means that we are continually improving.

Organize your thoughts. Take the time to think through how best to be organized and write down your plan. Label file drawers and shelves if it helps keep things where they belong.

Stick to your plan. It takes discipline to work a system once it's been developed, so be determined not to allow disorganization to stand in your way from accomplishing your goals.

Learn to Focus

Sometimes it seems as if *all* of us are suffering from attention deficit disorder, doesn't it? It's so easy to get sidetracked from what our main focus needs to be. While it is true that we need a five-minute breather every thirty minutes or so to stay alert, there are some ways we can stay focused, which keeps us on task getting the job done.

Determine your peak performance times. Every person has a natural body rhythm with peaks and valleys. Many people claim to be morning people, while others are night owls. Have you ever paid attention to what time of day you seem most productive? This would be your peak time. I once taught at a school where the wise principal tried his best to allow us to teach our toughest classes during our daily peak performance time. It allowed for better problem-solving ability, mental and physical energy, and creativity.

Schedule your most difficult tasks during your peak performance time. If you know that your sugar and energy level dip around 3 P.M. (which is quite common), don't schedule stressful decision-making meetings during this time. Perhaps you get that second wind just before four. Schedule tough assignments then. Most of us will be more productive first thing in the morning if we've had a good night's sleep and a nutritious breakfast.

Tackle your most difficult items first. Sometimes for the sake of getting to cross items off of a to-do list, people navigate toward the easy, less time-consuming chores first. However, it may be better to tackle the hardest project first during your peak performance time. Then, as your interest and energy dissipate, you can still probably get through the easier items and be relieved that they don't tax you as much.

Remove all distractions. Distractions come in many forms: interruptions, background music, an undone project, room temperature, even uncomfortable clothing. Whatever your frustrating distraction, try to get rid of it so that you aren't preoccupied thinking of or dealing with it. You will certainly be able to focus better.

Set incremental deadlines with end times. When I'm on deadline to write a book, I look at the whole calendar, beginning with when I can begin the book and when it's due at the publisher. If it's a three-month project and supposed to end up at two hundred pages, I divide all of the possible working days I can give it into the number of pages due. I then know how many pages per day need to get written to stay on time.

Then, I look at my daily appointment calendar and try to schedule several hours of concentrated writing time during each writing day. If, at the end of that time, I don't make my daily page quota, I know that I'm either going to have to work beyond what I'd scheduled that day or try to find another date when appointments can be postponed to give me additional time.

Any project can be broken into increments with deadlines. But it takes a lot of planning at the beginning of the project and the ability to actually focus on the assignment once the time comes to concentrate.

The Dreaded Meeting

Try "A Baker's Dozen" when planning a meeting.

Invite only those directly involved. Don't waste the time of those who are only involved in the fringe of your topic. Perhaps a copy of the meeting minutes is all they need to "stay in the loop."

Start on time at an odd time (9:28). This will get them there by 9:30.

Consider a "stand up" meeting. People get more done in less time because they can't get comfortable or sleepy by sitting.

Schedule meetings before another appointment, just before lunch, or just before quitting time. You'll be amazed at how little chitchat goes on when attendees are eager to get down to business so they won't be late out the door.

Provide an agenda. It's very helpful to provide this agenda before the meeting so that minds can be prepared for the issues at hand.

Designate a stopping time for each agenda item. Then, several minutes before the stopping time, summarize the agenda item and wind down the discussion.

Assign a person to be responsible for organizing items for the agenda. When creating an agenda beforehand, allow for feedback so that important additional items don't get overlooked.

Put the plush chairs in the front of the room if you want to fill the front first.

If the group gets stuck on a topic, table it by stopping and assigning someone to research it. He or she should be directed to report back about it at the next meeting or submit a written memo to each person who attended the meeting.

If the agenda is lengthy, assign different people to research and report on each item and make recommendations. They, in turn, become the experts to whom all questions can be addressed.

Send out a summary or meeting minutes within seventy-eight hours of the meeting. This clarifies any muddy issues while still fresh in everyone's mind.

Ten minutes before it is time to end the meeting, provide a brief summary and wind it up.

Clarify any action steps that have been assigned and when the deadline is for accomplishing those tasks. This can be included in the meeting minutes as well.

Meetings are two-edged swords: they interrupt our focus on ongoing projects and many times generate an even heavier workload for us. However, meetings do allow us opportunity for communication and clarification which can save time, motivate, and assist us in completing our task.

Be a "Contrarian"

Finally, an easy way to save time is to be a "contrarian." That is, be a person who does things at the opposite time that most people do.

Drive during nonpeak hours. A friend of ours who lives and works in the Detroit area figured out one day that if he leaves the office at five, with rush hour traffic, he gets home at 6:30. However, if he leaves at 5:45, after rush hour traffic, he still gets home at 6:30. Those forty-five minutes have ended up being very productive for him since most employees have left and the phones aren't ringing. Each day he looks forward to that chunk of time when he can really get things done.

Batch and piggyback. If you feel as if you have a million errands to run on all sides of town, stop to think about which things can be done at the same time in the same part of town. Batch together all like tasks, then begin your journey at the farthest point from your home or office. If you run out of time, you are working your way back to home base.

Christmas shop in the off-season. Those women who have most of their shopping done by July have shopped good sales and not had to contend with inclement weather, busy malls, or traffic tie-ups. These are the women who actually have time to bake during the holiday season.

Dine before the crowds. There is one particular restaurant that we have never tried because there is always an hour wait before we can be seated, and a line of people waiting for tables is strung outside the building. We know that if we could just get ourselves there before the crowds, we'd be able to enjoy the wonderful experience as well. Early dining also allows for taking advantage of the early-bird specials, so we can save time and money just by scheduling an early out-to-dinner meal.

Use office equipment during lunch, or before or after hours. A couple of places I've worked had limited fax sites and it seemed almost impossible to send out a fax without waiting for several who were already standing in line. I finally learned to batch all faxes together and send them all out together either after hours or before hours the next day.

Automate when possible. One company's office slogan was "Use your head so you don't have to use your feet." Thus, automatic deposit for checks becomes very appealing since you don't have to physically handle, sign, take to the bank, and wait in line to deposit them.

Avoid the bank on Friday. Those folks who have not yet caught on to direct check deposit clog up the bank drive-through and teller windows. Noon of any day is also a busy time at many banks, so be a contrarian and don't be seen there with the crowd.

Use the "surge mode." Think of an electrical outlet when there is an electrical surge. Lots of power surges through the lines in a short amount of time. You can get more done if you do a lot in a short amount of time that is uninterrupted. It is said that a writer who is interrupted takes twenty minutes to get back into the groove of the piece again. By surging uninterrupted, more work can get accomplished.

Make use of down time. One of my seminar attendees was bemoaning the fact that she was the neighborhood taxi driver: she chauffeured kids to dance, to soccer, to piano, to doctor's appointments, and on and on and on. What a waste of time, she lamented. I asked her what it was she wanted to get done during those drive and wait times. Well, she needed to balance her checkbook, finish research on a project, and read. It had never occurred to her that she could take these things along and make use of her down time.

Submit your time to God. Psalm 31:15 reminds us that "My times are in your hands." We can think we're managing our time wisely, but if our activity is not centered around the Lord's will for us, it is in vain.

As James 4:13-15 explains: "Now listen, you who say, 'Today or tomorrow we will go to this or that city, spend a year there, carry on business and make money.' Why, you do not even know what will happen tomorrow. What is your life? You are mist that appears for a little while and then vanishes. Instead, you ought to say, 'If it is the Lord's will, we will live and do this or that.'"

That kinda puts things in perspective, doesn't it? We can be involved in a whirlwind of activity—and think we're getting a lot done. But if we are not trying to accomplish the goals set before us by God, the time we've invested brings back no return. It is useless and worthless.

Those 86,400 Seconds

Keep in mind these issues as you decide how to spend that daily deposit of 86,400 seconds:

- Does your activity and attitude glorify God?

- Does your activity accomplish God's will and His goals for your life?

- Does your activity accentuate eternal rather than temporal values?

- Have you prayed about and submitted the spending of your time today to Him?

We have only the present time to spend. "Days that are past are gone forever, and those that are to come may not come to you. Therefore, enjoy today without regretting the loss of the past, or depending too much on that which is not yet here. This instant is yours, the next still belongs to futurity, and you do not know what it may bring forth."[4]

Perhaps there is a reason that we call today the present. It truly is a gift from God.

Father, we commit the way we spend our time to You. May each activity be time invested in Your eternal kingdom. Amen.

Everything Would Be Just Fine If I Didn't Have to Deal with All These Difficult People and Handle All These Complications! Preventing Problems and Dealing with Difficulties

Preventing Problems

Mother's Day gave my mom and me some time to reminisce about our family heritage. We lamented the fact that her mother (a sweet, patient, kind, and godly woman) suffered a stroke caused from high blood pressure when she was only in her fifties. The result was legal blindness in both eyes, which she graciously dealt with until her death at age eighty. Had today's technology been available to her then, one daily dose of a high blood pressure medication, a pill one-quarter the size of an aspirin, could have prevented this sad, debilitating condition. What a blessing it would have been if the preventive medicine had been available to her.

Today we have available to us many cures and solutions; shouldn't it follow that a little preventive medicine would eliminate many illnesses? Sadly, even when the preventive is available, it is often ignored until the problem becomes insurmountable. I've had friends who suffered from depression and stopped taking the medication prescribed to treat the illness. The results were disastrous and may have been prevented—broken relationships, incomprehensible emotional pain, and, yes, even suicide. How many heart attacks could be prevented just by practicing weight, exercise, and diet control? How many cancers could be prevented from spreading by early detection?

For years I complained that someone would be killed at a dangerous intersection near our house. Neighbors pleaded with the township to put up a stoplight, but the request was denied since no one had ever suffered a serious accident there. Then, one beautiful spring day toward the end of his senior year in high school, a young man was killed at this intersection. Today a four-way stop controls the traffic, but every time I wait my turn to proceed through this intersection, my stomach sickens knowing that his death might have been prevented.

It would seem logical, just like taking preventive medicine, that leaders would put into practice methods that would circumvent serious conflict, doesn't it? Yet, unfortunately, preventable problems still run rampant in our churches, schools, corporations, and homes.

As Christian women affecting our sphere of influence, we have a responsibility to be *proactive* in *preventing problems*! Problems and difficulties rob our time, sap our strength and divert us from productivity. Prevention involves:

- Forward thinking and planning

- Activity designed to prevent the onset of disaster

- Commitment and follow-through

It will come as no surprise to you, since we've already spent three chapters dealing with developing communication skills, that honest, timely communication is the cornerstone of preventing problems. This is true within any family unit, church group, educational institution, or corporate entity. When I see an organization suffering lack of morale, lack of respect, lack of enthusiasm, and lack of direction, I know that something is wrong with the leadership. Every activity, action, and attitude trickles down the ranks from leadership.

If you are in a position to develop and initiate these problem-preventing techniques in your area of influence, it's likely that you will embrace and enjoy this chapter. If, however, you are serving leadership that is not practicing these procedures, you will be frustrated by the things outside of your circle of influence.

My advice is to keep in mind that you do not need to wear a leadership title to lead. You can practice these preventive skills and make a noticeable difference where you are, even if leadership does not make a practice of listening to employees or communicating clearly with them. Also, take note of the things you have no control over that could be improved and vow that you will make better decisions when you are in a position to do so.

Internal Communication

As we've discussed, communication is a two-way street. Good leadership initiates the communication and invites workers—or family members—to respond and communicate back. Effective internal communication motivates workers and keeps up their morale, wards off rumors before they begin, and gains the loyalty of those she is responsible for.

Let's look at how to prevent low morale and lack of motivation.

Lead by Example

If we notice the boss repeatedly arriving at the office an hour after office hours begin, taking a two-hour, non-business-related lunch, and leaving an hour before quitting time, how do you think the office staff will respond? Typically people will either develop a cynical attitude about it or follow the example.

I could tell scores of true stories about leaders who lead by example (which they do whether they are trying to or not). They either build morale or crush it. People instinctively want leaders that they can look up to, emulate, and respect. The leader's conduct determines the work ethic, morality, and general attitudinal atmosphere of the whole organization. Several ways you can lead by example include:

Be willing to make sacrifices, and you will see those around you following your example.

Determine that you will listen to the ideas of others without criticism or passing judgment and you will discover that the exchange of ideas will freely flow between you and your sphere of influence.

Take the first steps toward initiating a smile and positive attitude, and you will see your image reflected brightly in those around you.

Be the first and last to say thanks. Saying thanks costs nothing yet means so much. Expressing our thanks and appreciation can take on the form of spoken words, written notes, and kind gestures. Even more effective are a few words of public praise. Why? I don't know about you, but when the teacher used to read from an A paper in the classroom, and it wasn't mine, I worked all the harder to write a better paper the next time so that mine might be the one read and applauded.

Likewise, a quick e-mail, humorous card, letter of recommendation for her file, or an inexpensive bouquet of flowers all send the message that she is appreciated. It also reminds her of the qualities of the giver of these good gifts, which she *will* emulate. As we have noted before, we tend to mirror the leader. "Speak kind words and you will hear kind echoes," as Benjamin Franklin said.

Reward Appropriately

I've been a little frustrated with the latest academic paradigm that views competition and reward as a negative thing. Several school systems in our area won't even conduct spelling bees anymore for fear of hurting the ego of the child less prepared or equipped to compete. The concern is that if one child is rewarded for his or her performance, it will be unfair to the other children.

My question is: what, then, is the motivation for students to excel? It is human nature to be motivated through reward and recognition. Even more so, adults respond and are motivated by the incentive of reward. If it weren't so, we would not promise commissions based upon sales or bonuses dependent upon production. Healthy competition between sales representatives, siblings, or Sunday School kids is fun and invigorating.

Reward is the result of self-discipline and hard work. Hmm, two other traits that trickle down from leadership. Leaders have a responsibility to demonstrate self-discipline and hard work and the privilege of rewarding it when they see it practiced.

Capitalize on People's Strengths

Let's face it, we *all* have weaknesses and the best way to allow someone to fail and be frustrated is to keep her in her area of weakness.

Several years ago I worked for a few months as a temporary employee for a large furniture company. The first job they gave me was to spend eight hours per day pulling out staples from documents that were being prepared for microfiche. I actually cried at my desk for the whole first day I was there wondering why a recording artist, writer, and communications trainer was given this awful assignment.

To her credit, the supervisor realized that someone else could do this job and that the quality of the department would be enhanced if she capitalized on my strengths and experience. The idea is to assign people jobs that they do *best*. Before long the supervisor assigned me to learn about the entire state-of-the-art communications technology of their plant and allowed me to put together a training manual on the proper telephone techniques that their customer service people should follow. I was *elated*. I was happy with my assignment and the department benefited from the manual.

Do you see wonderful people around you who are being less productive, and certainly less content, because they are working a job at their frustration level? Within our TimeOut for Women! organization, there have been times when I could have "wadded up and thrown away" an individual who either worked for us or was a volunteer, but first asked myself what her strengths were. In fact, I often ask our workers what they feel they do best and what they enjoy doing most.

One woman might admit that she's not organized and doesn't keep great records, but look how good she is with people and how effective she is with phone work. Let's allow her to excel in what she does best. She has an eye for numbers and accounts, but doesn't do well when dealing with people. That's okay. Let her organize the behind the scenes technical schedules. She's a creative person who loves to write. Keep her (and me!) away from the accountant's books! You get the idea. Everyone wins when we capitalize on a person's strengths—she does what she does best and we enjoy higher productivity.

Although Paul was talking about spiritual gifts, in Romans 12 and 1 Corinthians 12 he makes the case that the body has many parts and each of them provides an important function necessary for the proper working of the whole. The same is true in our working or ministry environment. Each woman brings a strength and talent with her; therefore she must be given the opportunity to function within the confines of her greatest potential.

Clarify Expectations and Evaluation

I was once asked to take over the temporary directorship in a department while a search was going on to fill the position. I agreed, but only under the condition that a general job description be given to me and the criteria for evaluation. Can you believe that these things were denied? I turned it down. No way was I going to walk into a situation in which I was given no direction and not a clue as to what was expected of me.

I'm not suggesting that we must always outline a detailed job description. Sometimes too much detail and not enough flexible latitude can kill the effectiveness of our people. However, general guidelines and constant affirmation of those is essential for us as we lead by example.

Stay in Constant Contact

Here's a way to deflate motivation: don't stay involved. People not only need some accountability, but they embrace it. We don't have to be looking over their shoulders all the time, but it's good to say, "Hey, whatcha got going on today?" or "Is there anything I can do to assist you in this?" "What are the things that are frustrating you with this project?"

We have a unique operation at TimeOut for Women! in that we have seven paid staff and over three hundred volunteers that make this ministry work. What complicates the situation even more is that these women are spread out over five states. Yet, through the use of e-mail, faxes, snail mail, and the telephone, we stay in touch daily.

We often include the entire staff from each state in the discussion of a particular issue—even if it doesn't directly affect them at the time, because eventually it may. Why? First of all so they can be in prayer for their fellow staff. Second, so they can be a part of the creative brainstorm in finding a solution. Third, when they face the same predicament at their location, they already have a solution well in hand.

Staying in touch takes time and thoughtfulness, but is the best way to unify a team, clarify misunderstandings, and solve problems. All of us together are smarter than just one standing alone.

Prevent Harmful Rumors from Developing and Spreading

The rumor mill can tear down walls of communication faster than a wrecking ball can demolish a one-story building. Preventing rumors from beginning and spreading in the first place is the best offense in the game of effective internal communications.

Be Aware of Appearances (Point of View)

The Bible tells us that we should abstain even from the appearance of evil (1 Thess. 5:22).

I used to teach a class called "Art of the Motion Picture." In it we studied plots, camera angles, characterization, and lighting. One particular film I always showed at the beginning of the term was called *Point of View*. It was a murder mystery presented six different ways through the eyes of six different witnesses.

From the viewpoint of the cleaning lady, it appeared that the victim's boyfriend had committed her murder. From the viewpoint of the man living in the apartment next door, it was obvious that it was the cleaning lady who committed the murder. The deliveryman was sure that he saw the jealous girlfriend leaving the apartment and that she had to be the murderer.

The point (of view) here is obvious: we draw conclusions based upon the information available to us. Since none of the characters actually witnessed the murder, they made assumptions and conclusions based upon the limited facts they were exposed to—just what they could "see."

Here's a true story about the danger of appearances and point of view. A friend of ours got out of his car to run into the drugstore while holding a white ink pen in his hand, similar to the way a cigarette is held. One of his colleagues, driving by, glanced at our friend and made the logical assumption that he was smoking, which was prohibited by the nonprofit organization we all worked for. This mistaken assumption caused quite a stir regarding the future employment of our friend.

As women who influence, we must guard well against even the appearance of evil. Could our dinner meeting with a male salesman from our branch office be misinterpreted as an inappropriate relationship? Could our attendance at a controversial rally or concert suggest support for a cause that might not honor the Lord?

Sure, it's *wrong* for people to jump to conclusions and unjustly judge us, but they do it. Therefore, we need to make all attempts at abstaining from even the *appearance* of indiscretion.

One final bit of advice for us: Believe nothing of what you hear and only half of what you see. In John 7:24 Jesus instructs, "Stop judging by mere appearances, and make a right judgment." As we discovered in the film *Point of View*, appearances can be deceiving and if we want to come to a correct conclusion, we must have all of the correct facts before us first.

How to Prevent Disloyalty and Lack of Respect

Although we don't think of loyalty and respect as communication issues, they are attitudes that ultimately do control what we communicate. And they are the result of effective internal communication.

If we continue with the premise that people mirror their leadership, it follows that leadership must *first* commit acts of loyalty and respect if it hopes to receive the same in return.

Orchestrate the Timely Dissemination of Information

One way to squelch rumors before they begin is to develop a strategy to disseminate internal communications.

You too have certainly experienced rumors of cutbacks, rumors of layoffs, and rumors of resignation. It happens in the church, nonprofit organizations, and corporations. I attribute this unnecessary UNcontrol to two things:

The lack of confidentiality among leadership and

The lack of strategic planning to announce change.

I was once in charge of media relations for a nonprofit organization and received a phone call from the mayor in a nearby city. He wanted to know if it was true that our organization was closing one of our programs there.

Now, as media relations director, I should have been the first one privy to discussions about the closing so that I could be prepared for questions, or write a public comment release for the media.

Since I had heard nothing, I profusely denied the allegations and hung up. After some thought, however, I decided I better talk with the vice president to see if there was any truth to the rumor. When I approached him, he literally turned green. I don't know if it was an oversight or a calculated strategy to keep the news quiet, but I had totally been left out of the internal communication loop, which greatly affected our image in the external communication loop.

Furthermore, the "leak" was traced back to an employee who should have held the news confidential until a formal announcement was made. About a dozen jobs were on the line, so rumors only fueled the agony and anger of those fearing for their jobs.

Proper protocol could have prevented the miscommunication that ensued. What should have happened is this:

Leadership should have made the decision and committed to confidentiality.

Leadership should have informed the media relations person as to the facts and how those would be presented internally and externally.

Leadership should have met individually with each person whose job was affected by the change and asked for confidentiality until the cuts were announced.

Simultaneously, an internal announcement (either through e-mail or joint corporate meeting) and external press release (via fax or press conference) should have taken place.

All of this should have been planned ahead of time and orchestrated so that within one day, all *correct* information could be disseminated to all parties involved.

The mishandling of this announcement hurt—most of all—the people whose families depended upon this program for their income and self-esteem.

Yet they were the last to hear the news officially, while it was widely discussed in the rumor mill.

As we've already established, confidential lines of correct communication are a *must* in demonstrating loyalty and respect. Honesty about even the bad things is always the best policy.

Conduct Business and Relationships with Honesty and Integrity

I have the opportunity to travel with my husband on business several times each year. He has an adequate travel budget, but we have always felt that it would be dishonest to include my expenses under his account. So, each time I am on the road with him, he either pays separately for my meals and travel fees, or writes a check later to cover it. This small and honest gesture has spoken volumes to his support staff as to his integrity. The benefit for him is that his staff does not fudge on their expenses either. He has earned their loyalty and respect from just doing what is right.

Show Sincere Concern and Interest

How many times do we pass someone quickly in the hallway and insincerely huff, "How are ya?" and then walk away before she can even take a breath? This certainly is not a demonstration of sincere concern and interest. Conversely, we can't be the self-appointed in-house psychologist either, but there are times in leadership when it serves us and the organization best when we take note of the personal and professional issues our staff is dealing with. Effective leaders show compassion.

People can spot a phony miles away, so our interest must be genuine and heartfelt, or it won't be effective. If we hand concern and compassion over, it will be returned back.

Willingness to Listen

Another way leaders gain and maintain respect is through their willingness to listen. This does not mean that we solve all problems or even agree with the discussion. We all have a need to be heard (and, we hope, understood). Listening opens the doorway to loyalty.

Protection

We have an obligation to protect our staff, even when blame could be placed upon them. Sure, it would personally feel real good to me to say,

"Well, she sure blew it and it's all her fault!" However, what good will that do us as an organization? It destroys internal morale, trust, and loyalty—and demonstrates a fractured organization externally. We all lose: the individual, the organization, and our constituency.

Leaders are in a position to protect their people by maintaining a united front. If one in our department makes a big mistake, we all as a department take the rap. I take responsibility for my staff in the public arena. Therefore, I willingly take the blame for the mistake as if it were my own. I protect my people. And just like Jesus, I always give a second chance.

The result? When we protect our staff, they protect and defend us. This is the true essence of respect and loyalty.

Living a Lifestyle a "Cut Above"

Leaders are required to set a higher standard and live a cut above average. In fact, the higher you go in the ranks of leadership, the fewer "rights" you will have and the more responsibility you will shoulder. In its simplest form, this is servant leadership.

The leader who is able to live this higher lifestyle will quickly earn the respect and loyalty of her followers. No one said that leadership is easy. But leading by example, Christ's example, is the right way to lead.

External Communication

We've covered many issues that deal with the positive effects of proper internal communication and how it can prevent problems from becoming difficulties to deal with. Let's now take a look at how we can prevent problems by practicing correct external communication. This would include any situation where our organization touches the lives of those outside of our immediate staff or fellowship.

Every Employee Is Your Public Relations Director

Many times the only exposure an outsider has to our organization is through our work or volunteer force. Their opinions might be the only source of information an outsider has of our inside organization. Because of this, it's necessary for us to view each paid staff person, family member, or volunteer as a highly esteemed and valuable public relations director. This applies in our church situation, nonprofit corporations, and businesses.

As a communication trainer, I've taught at major automotive plants in

Michigan for both Ford and General Motors. I've also trained at plants that supplied parts to the larger companies. My classes have been a mixed bag, ranging from assembly line workers with third-grade educations to engineers who earned a Ph.D.

Within about the first ten minutes of class, I could discern the current buzz at that plant. Usually it was negative. After a while I just expected lack of morale, respect, and support of leadership as the prevalent attitude among those in my class.

However, when I was asked to train at what was then Prince Corporation (now Johnson Controls), I entered a whole new environment. The employees were actually satisfied and were the best public relations representatives the company could ask for. While my class was filled with men and women from every academic background and work experience, these folks were content with the company.

They displayed a unified spirit of cooperation that I didn't often see at other plants. They spoke highly of their superiors. There was a lightheartedness and fun sense of humor in the classroom, yet a serious approach to learn and apply my teaching.

Their satisfied attitudes led to improved productivity, fewer internal problems, and a company reputation that made (and still makes) the community proud. No amount of money poured into an advertising campaign could equal this type of endorsement. A satisfied employee equals positive external communication.

Ask the Dogs

Listen to the workers closest to the customer. This sounds simple and obvious, but you would be amazed at how many leaders overlook the importance of getting feedback from the person who works closest to the customer.

Countless women who are trying to get a women's group established in their church complain to me each year that they just can't get women to attend their activities. I ask them, "Have you asked your women what *they* want?" Most of the time, my answer is a blank stare.

This reminds me of a story Fred Smith shared at a leadership conference I attended years ago at Asbury College. He told us of a dog food company that had spent millions of dollars in researching the nutritional elements for a new dog food. It was an appealing color and had a wonderful aroma. Then, the marketing group got on board with the packaging and advertising to what had potential to be an incredible winner of a product.

They launched the campaign, which successfully drew in high sales as customers bought their first bag of this incredible dog food.

However, shortly after, sales dipped dramatically, and eventually the new product was a huge fizzle. The apparent reason? The dogs did not like the taste of the food. NOBODY ASKED THE DOGS!

In *Fresh Wind, Fresh Fire*, Jim Cymbala recalls conversations between some music publishers and his wife, Carol, who directs the Brooklyn Tabernacle Choir. The publishers pressed her for her secret writing formula so that they might be able to pattern their new music after it. Her response to them was that she spends time in prayer. Then, God inspires her with ideas that will speak and minister to her audiences. They just couldn't get it. Carol understands her congregation—in effect it's her customer. She listens to its needs, then responds with inspirational music to soothe, teach, and encourage it.[1]

What food should you serve in your restaurant? Ask the customer what she wants on the menu or listen to the servers. What clothing should you stock in your boutique? Ask shoppers what colors they like and what style. What song should you sing at church next Sunday? Ask people in your congregation what songs minister to them.

I would highly recommend your reading *The Soul of the Firm* by Bill Pollard, former CEO of ServiceMaster. One way ServiceMaster has prevented external problems is through listening to the worker closest to the customer. In fact, ServiceMaster has actually developed and patented new cleaning agents and gismos as a response to suggestions made by its employees.

Each year, regardless of title or position, each leader at ServiceMaster is expected to participate in training other employees and getting hands-on experience by working alongside even the lowliest (when it comes to job descriptions) of employees. It's called "We Serve" day and offers its leaders the opportunity to identify with the struggles of their workers, and perhaps provide them with innovative ways to solve problems.[2]

Think of the external public relations value this allows. What happens to the morale and respect of a coworker who is joined by a company VP in cleaning bugs off a Greyhound bus windshield, or working side-by-side cleaning a hospital room baseboard? Pretty awesome opportunity for servant leadership that will evoke, trust, respect, and loyalty. What better way to prevent external communication problems.

The Best Spokespersons Are Those "in the Know"

In other words, owners or top-level decision makers make the best spokespersons. Sometimes external communications can be bogged down by the very PR firm that's supposed to assist it. One such example comes from Robert Townsend in *Up the Organization*. When he was at Avis, he eliminated the entire public relations staff. He gave the telephone operators the names and telephone numbers of the top ten executives and they were told to find one of them to answer any questions the press might have.

The executives were given a framework (good internal communication) to work within, such as the type of questions to answer and what facts not to divulge. Let me quote here the rest of the story:

> This system worked well. Example. One day Ford Motor Company announced they were going directly into the rent a car business through any Ford dealer that wanted to. The *Wall Street Journal* phoned and was put through to the general manager of our rent a car division. Next day the front-page left-hand column was heavily salted with quotes from their conversation.
>
> Far down the page our competitor's VP of Public Relations had pulled off this coup: "A spokesman for the Hertz Corporation said they were studying the matter."[3]

Good internal communication can serve to brief a number of people in your organization so that at any time the same questions can be answered by a variety of people "in the know" which makes for great external communication. This cuts through the red tape of bureaucracy and empowers people to do their jobs.

Fail to Plan and You Plan to Fail

Preventing problems from arising in the first place hinges upon the ability of the leader to clearly see possible obstacles and opportunities. There is no magical crystal ball here; if the leader truly knows her product and customer (the product could be the Gospel and the customer her neighbor), she must develop a strategy for fulfilling the plan.

Importance of Casting Vision

You and I have both heard this phrase tossed around as the current leadership craze phrase. Just what does it mean, anyway?

Most of the dictionaries will define casting as *throwing*. One of the phrases used in the *Living Webster's* is "throw forth, as from within"[4] I really like that as it pertains to a leader casting vision. Our vision is that inner dream or revelation that allows us to see the possibilities, the solution, the direction that others may not. Casting vision requires us to throw our ideas out there so that others will trust the direction we want to send them.

Therefore, the first step in planning must be the ability to see clearly which direction we need to go. Not everyone has the ability to see the whole forest; some people see just the trees.

Helping People See the Vision

"Without vision the people perish" (Prov. 29:18, paraphrased). Vision is a picture in the mind of the leader of how things can and should be. Max Dupree says, "We can teach ourselves to see things the way they are. Only with vision can we begin to see things the way they can be."[5]

As leaders, we have a responsibility to make ears into eyes so that others too can catch our vision and see what we see. John Maxwell maintains that "People buy into the leaders, then the vision."[6] In other words, they first trust the leader. Bob Briner says, "Good leaders have a vision; better leaders share a vision."[7] Our responsibility is to provide a road map of sorts so that our people have a plan that, if followed, will get them to their destination.

Clear vision and a strong strategy for fulfilling the plan can prevent problems from cropping up. Of course, it would be totally naive to think that our world could be void of problems. Forward planning can prevent some problems from taking root, however difficulties will always be a part of the equation. Since difficulties are a reality, how should we deal with them when they do arise so that we are honoring God and exemplifying quality leadership? Here are some suggestions.

Dealing with Difficulties

Whether you are a leader in your home or the president of a major corporation, problems will emerge and you will be forced to deal with difficulties. Take heart! These can offer incredible opportunities for the growth and development of character and stamina.

Much of our success in dealing with difficulties depends upon the attitude we decide to adopt. Yes, attitude *is* a *choice*. We can choose to calmly react or to fly off the handle. Have you ever set a goal in mind for the type of responder you want to be when facing difficulties? Yes, you read it correctly. Have you ever thought to pre-plan your response in a crisis situation? We train doctors how to handle emergencies. Firefighters train for the unexpected. Why shouldn't leaders work to become equipped to handle difficult issues and circumstances that will most certainly come their way?

Having been involved some with theater in high school and college, then teaching drama, I often will think: if there were a script written for me to follow in this situation—one where the playwright knew the ending, how would I act? Now don't get me wrong. I don't act a predetermined role that I've created. As you've gathered throughout this book, the premise of my life is to be sincere and genuine—in order to gain trust, respect, and loyalty.

However, as leaders, we must develop a mature, biblically based strategy for dealing with difficulties so that when they arise, we can face them with confidence. When I began teaching, I determined that I would never cry in front of a classroom of students as had so many of my own high school teachers. I must admit that there were several times over the years when I ended up at a break crying in the faculty lounge, but it would have been disastrous to my authority in the classroom had the students felt that they had worn me down to that point.

Similarly, as TimeOut for Women! has grown and evolved, I've determined never to lose my temper or show outward anger toward any of our participants, staff members, or vendors. And there are times when unfair, unkind, or dishonest situations could give just cause for me to explode in a fit of justified rancor. What good does it do? After everything has settled, and things always do settle, the only memory a non-Christian might have of me is one of yelling and screaming, not lovingly building the kingdom of God. Which kind of image do I want to draw attention to?

Here's a story that illustrates my point. We try to set conference dates at least two years in advance since many speakers are booked that far ahead. I always wait until everything is in writing, at least through a memo with a confirmed venue, before planning the event.

One year the arena we had scheduled to use called to tell me that our date had been given to another group, thinking that ours was a flexible event. Here I had waited two years for these six presenters to become available, and now I had no venue.

In a split second, I had to make a choice whether I would follow the imaginary script I had written to follow in a crisis, or whether I would allow emotion to dictate my actions.

Knowing that I was working with non-Christians, I wanted to be as Christlike as possible. So, I assertively, but kindly, expressed my dismay at what this situation meant to us—possibly canceling, but added that I would trust God to lead me in the right direction.

In the meantime, a large church invited us to use its facility. *Hey, look how God works*, I thought. I felt then that I had a righteous justification to lambaste the arena for the situation it put me in by writing scathing letters to the chamber of commerce, Better Business Bureau, and to the local newspaper. I drafted a good one. Oh, man, did it just hurl the truth smack dab in their faces with the promise of poor recommendations and more scathing reports. I finished it, set it aside, and felt nauseous.

I then met my husband for lunch, where we continued discussion of this heated issue. In the middle of the meal my cell phone rang. It was a church representative apologetically relaying to me that it was not going to be able to host us after all. So, here I was, with a great lineup of speakers and musicians and no place that could accommodate the thousands of women who had signed up to attend.

Actually, my husband and I made an attitude decision right then that we would just shrug it off, enjoy our lunch together, and put it all in God's hands to resolve. I threw away my letter to the arena and spent the next week in prayer—not desperate prayer, just talking to God about what He wanted me to do.

One week from the day that we were told we couldn't use the church facility I received a fax from an arena spokesperson apologizing for its mistake and informing me that it had moved the other group and the arena was ours as had been originally agreed upon.

Now, how do you think this story would have ended had I actually sent that insulting, angry letter? Do you think the arena managers would have gone to the bother of moving the other group's date? And how would I have looked in their eyes? What would their opinion of TimeOut for Women! have been? Or, by reflection, Christians.

As it has turned out, we held that conference at the arena and God's Spirit moved mightily, as He always does when given the platform. And, we discovered that the female employees at the arena attended our conference and were touched. In fact, now many make plans to work at our event whenever we travel to their town so they can be a part of an inspirational experience. Our prayer is that they will come to know the Lord as their personal Savior as a result.

Well, I wish I could brag that I handle every difficulty as sterling, but I'm still learning too. So, let's just try to scratch the surface on some of the issues that will come your way, and mine, and cite some creative ways to deal with these difficulties.

Decision Making

If only making decisions were as easy as it seemed in Old Testament days. Take a peek at Exodus 28:15-30. Here God tells how to fashion the breastpiece for Aaron, the high priest. It was exquisite. Rubies, topaz, turquoise, sapphires, and emeralds were mounted in gold filigree settings. Chains of pure gold were braided like rope to connect it to the ephod.

Then, over the heart of the breastpiece, there was a small pocket where Aaron was to keep the Urim and Thummim. It is thought that these were sacred lots that he would draw out when making decisions. If he brought out the Urim, the answer was *no*. If he drew out the Thummim, the answer from God was *yes*.

It's interesting that drawing lots for decision making was very typical of the Old Testament followers of God. Proverbs 16:33 declares that "The lot is cast into the lap, but its every decision is from the Lord."

When we journey into the New Testament, however, it is interesting that once the Holy Spirit is given, first-century Christians stop the practice of casting lots to learn God's decisions. Acts 1:26 tells us that after casting lots, Matthias was chosen to be added to the eleven apostles. In Acts 2, the Holy Spirit descends. In Acts 6:1-6, the apostles again add to their number, this time choosing seven. Nowhere do we read that lots were cast for this decision. We conclude that it was the discernment of the Holy Spirit that led them to the correct decisions.

I want to share with you a step-by-step process that may assist you in making decisions, keeping in mind we have the Holy Spirit as our supernatural partner in this.

Determine Whether It Is a Moral or an Amoral Decision

This may be stating the obvious, but I can recount numerous examples in which someone has struggled through a decision that was so obvious from biblical standards, trying to justify an immoral choice. For instance, deciding what suit works best for an interview is an amoral decision. Deciding whether to fudge on the truth in the accounting of a sale is a moral decision. The Bible is very clear about what is right and wrong.

Deciding whether to take a promotion, or move to a new city, is likely an amoral decision, unless you are choosing to move where there are fewer moral restrictions on an immoral lifestyle. The point is, of course, that moral decisions have already been addressed in God's Word, and we can avoid all kinds of other problems if we follow His law. Other decisions such as finances, personnel, location, promotion, or resignation may have moral consequences, but they are not as obvious. What does God want us to do? Well, let's ask Him by allowing Him to have first and final authority in our decision.

Take It to God First

Yes, you've prayed about it, but what good does that do anyway? It's just you praying to Someone out there that can't be seen or touched. God can't really talk back to us anyway, can He? Or does He? If He does, how might we receive His message?

I would propose to you that there are at least five ways that God speaks to us:

His Word

God's Word teaches us rules to live by that protect and provide for us. I've learned to look at these not as the "Thou Shalt Nots," but the "You Can Dos." I've recounted and expanded upon just the Ten Commandments at the end of this chapter, but there are many more teachings in the Word as to what we *can* do.

The other wisdom gained from God's Word comes from reading about the examples of successes and failures in decision making. Look at the mess Saul made of things as the anointed king of Israel. Analyze the mistakes King David made as a father and husband, or the wise decisions he often made in battle. Study the life of Jesus to see how He did the right and perfect thing. God's Word is a storehouse of examples that we can base our decisions upon today.

Prayer

Prayer is not just a one-way street where our thoughts travel up the avenue to be parked at the throne of God. No. Prayer is like any other type of communication in which there is a message sent, a message understood, and a response made.

God's message may likely come from His Word, but it may also come from that still small voice inside. Like me, you might experience times in prayer when an idea comes to mind that is not a typical thought for you, but one that helps you make a decision.

Whatever the process, prayer is a significant part of Christians' decision-making.

Discernment

You may want to call this women's intuition because it's hard to define. It's an awareness that something is not right, or that something is right. It's that gut feeling that tells you to trust or not trust someone. When I believe God gives me discernment about something, I try to do some fact finding to back it up so that I'm not running on emotion. When I get all the facts, I realize that the discernment God gave me was correct.

Godly Counsel

From the very beginning, God said that it was "not good for man to be alone" (Gen. 2:18). Each of us needs a helper, no matter what our circumstance. In the Old Testament, the twelve tribes of Israel each had its gift and function within the nation. In the New Testament, Jesus chose twelve disciples as His inner core to be trained for His service and to support Him in His ministry. Why, then, would we ever consider making significant decisions in solitude?

Even as we go back to the Scripture in Acts 6, we see that there was a problem with the Jewish widows being overlooked in the distribution of food. Before a decision was made as to how to deal with the problem, verse two says that "the Twelve gathered all the disciples together," and they discussed together how to proceed. All of us together are wiser than one alone.

Peace

Finally, there is great peace when we are in the center of God's will. Romans 8:6 says, "the mind controlled by the Spirit is life and peace." 1 Corinthians 14:33 reminds us that "God is not a God of disorder but of peace." Part of Zechariah's song in Luke 1:78-79 encourages us that "the tender mercy of our God [will] guide our feet into the path of peace."

Peace gives us freedom from worry and allows us to sleep at night. Peace tells us when we have made the best decision.

Collect All the Facts

Someone once told me that when you research and gather all of the facts, the decision just about slaps you in the face. When I look back at decisions I've regretted, I often ask myself if I would have made the same decision again with the amount of information I had. Usually, I would. However, we can certainly avoid costly mistakes by getting all the facts.

One word of warning here: There are *always* three sides. Their side, your side, and the truth. It's so tempting to allow one side to sway the scales, so give a decision time, if you can, and make sure that you've got the correct facts—all the facts.

In their book *Managing Your Time*, Ted Engstrom and Alec MacKenzie suggest keeping in mind the following advice regarding decision making:

- Don't make the decision under stress

- Don't make snap decisions

- Don't drag your feet

- Consult other people

- Don't try to anticipate everything

- Don't be afraid of making a wrong decision

- Once the decision is made, go on to something else[8]

Problem Solving

Closely aligned with making wise decisions is the issue of solving problems. Here's a good definition of a problem: It is a problem if I can do something about it. If I can't, it's just a fact of life; it is out of my circle of control. True problem solving gets at the root of the issue and cures the source; it doesn't just put a bandage on the symptom. Just as in the weeding process, it is often a painful and time-consuming endeavor. However, a problem left unattended is a garden allowed to be overrun with weeds. Eventually the bad chokes out the good so that there appears to be no fruit left in the garden.

A leader should never be so arrogant as to give the impression that she knows *the* best solution. The most effective problem-solving method involves the whole team. Okay, so we are way over budget. What has to go? Who can be moved? How can we improve sales? What are all the possibilities? Processing to get to the solution involves the whole team so that each person takes ownership in the final decision.

The problem-solving process should:

- Identify the problem

- Prioritize the problem

- Define the problem

- Select people to help in the problem-solving process

- Collect problem causes

- Collect problem-solving solutions

- Prioritize and select the best solutions

- Implement the best solution

- Evaluate the solution

Following these steps may take just a few hours, a couple of days, or many months. However, this process will eventually weed out the problems and provide acceptable solutions.

Crisis

We've already discussed how proper communication can ward off a possible crisis, but there will be times when we must deal with a crisis. If it happens, here are some words of wisdom to get you through:

- Identify all audiences affected by the crisis (internal and external)

- Communicate only those things that are a certainty (avoid speculation)

- Deal face-to-face and one-on-one

- Don't lie about anything, but don't feel compelled to divulge information before its time

- Convey the impression that you are accessible and communicative

- Don't comment on hypothetical situations

- Communicate bad news all at one time

- Obtain feedback from internal and external through research and focus groups

- Monitor and evaluate the change

- Admit any mistakes and apologize for them

- Inform all employees at the same time

- Remember that employees equal public relations

- Use multiple media for communicating change (e-mail, memo, fax, simultaneous meetings)

Handling a crisis properly requires wisdom, proper strategy, and correct follow-through. Most people will keep a good attitude toward you and the crisis if they feel you are being honest and fair in the way you divulge information and handle the sensitive issues.

Criticism

Being criticized comes with the territory if you are doing anything that is contributing to society. Much of it is unfair and unjustified, but if you are in a position to influence, you will be criticized.

On the other side of the issue, there will be times when we are forced to deal with a situation and criticize the work or behavior of someone else. This is no fun either. How do we tactfully get our message across and still maintain a Christlike attitude?

How to give it:

- Do it privately

- Do it as soon as possible

- Speak to one issue at a time

- Don't repeat a point after making it (rub it in)

- Deal only with actions a person can change

- Avoid sarcasm

- Don't use the words *always* or *never*

- Present criticisms as suggestions or questions

- Don't apologize for the confrontation

- Sandwich in compliments (compliment/confront/compliment)

How to take it:

I don't handle criticism lightly; maybe you are like that too. Criticism is difficult for me to hear because I try so hard not to offend in the first place. Of course, anyone who accepts any type of leadership responsibility *will* be criticized. Let's see how some of our contributors have learned to respond to criticism:

Florence Littauer: "If someone criticizes me to my face, I just simply say, 'Thank you for bringing that to my attention. I really appreciate it.' If they send a letter, I may skim it, but because I have so many positive people to respond to, I usually don't write back."

Madeline Manning Mims: "It hurts, but it's not the end of the world. Let the Lord fight that battle for where I am weak, He is strong!"

Robin Koop: "I ask God for His wisdom. I realize that I'm just human and need guidance to become a better person—using the talents that God has given me."

Kay DeKalb Smith: "I examine the criticism to see if there is something I need to learn—or if I have been blind in some area. I seek council of godly people to find out if I need to change, then I try to communicate to my critic to let them know what God revealed to me."

Elisa Morgan: "After bristling a bit(!) I listen for truth. I tend to take responsibility for things I didn't even do, so I have to watch this and carefully let go of a wrongful accusation, as well as a very human desire that everyone like me."

Barbie Cooper: "I don't usually put out brush fires; I usually ignore them. They eventually smolder out and die."

Carol Kent: "Many times criticism comes because someone misunderstood my method, my material, or my motive. It hurts even when there is a small amount of truth in it. I have to first admit any wrong on my part. If there is none, I must let go of it and forgive the person. Most people are critical of others because the only way they can elevate themselves is to put someone else down. When I realize that the critical person is a hurting person, it helps me to forgive that person and to eliminate bitterness or anger."

Millie Dienert: "I accept the criticism rather than getting angry and rejecting it. In all criticism there can be something *worth* looking at."

Liz Curtis Higgs: "How I handle criticism—hmm, you mean *after* I rant and rave and carry on? (Just kidding!) First I ask myself if there is a grain of truth (maybe even a bucket of truth) in their critical words. If so, I learn from it and consider the lesson a blessing. And tell them so. If their words are critical but *not* constructive or even accurate, I remind myself of how much Christ suffered on my behalf. This small slight is *nothing* compared to that. I swallow my pride and move on. Often I have to share my hurt privately with my husband or close friend so that I can process it."

Babbie Mason: "Even if criticism is constructive it can sometimes be hurtful and discouraging. So I try my best to weigh it. If the criticism is constructive, I look at it objectively, believing there is always room for improvement in what I do. I take into consideration that the person offering the criticism may be better informed or may have more experience than I. This type of criticism is helpful in honing skills."

Zig Ziglar puts the criticism of critics in perspective by encouraging us not to "be distracted by criticism. Remember—the only taste of success some people have is when they take a bite out of you."

Mike Murdock, in *Leadership Secrets of Jesus,* maintains that "Critics are spectators, not players. Critical people are disappointed people. Disillusioned people. Unfocused people. They are hurting inside. They build their life trying to destroy others."[10] Notice that Jesus ignored many of His critics to give His attention to those things that were a part of His mission.

Critics are not The Enemy, and might very well bring to our attention possibilities we had not considered before. It's important for us to separate our *self* from the *behavior* that is being criticized. Even if we have made a mistake or decision that lacked judgment, it does not make us bad. If several people bring to our attention the same issue, we must adopt an attitude of appreciation that they cared enough to mention it. If the criticism is unfounded, we must learn to walk away from it.

The Positive Effects of Problems and Difficulties

Yes, there are positives that result from difficulties. You've heard it said that a pearl would never be created if it weren't for the irritation of the sand within the smooth lining of the oyster. Problems sometimes become our greatest blessing because they challenge our creativity and lead us into necessary adjustments.

Problems Are Agents of Change Within an Organization

Pick up any book written by a corporate president or church leader and it will be confirmed that a changing organization is the key to meeting needs of people within and outside of an organization. I would venture to say that pastors have seen a drastic change in some of the counseling issues they see today compared with what they dealt with twenty years ago. Why, AIDS was just being researched then, the divorce rate was not nearly as high as it is today, and personal computers were just a thought for the future, and no one had even considered what the Internet would become.

Instead of resisting the change that problems initiate, we must learn to embrace change and make it our closest ally.

Problems Give Us Experience That Will Help Avoid Future Problems

I like the old phrase, "Bit once, shame on them; bit twice, shame on you!" We all get bitten now and then with a new experience, but if we get bitten twice by the same circumstance, we haven't learned anything.

Let's face each painful problem as a learning tool that will help us avoid future problems.

Problems Allow for Creative Exchange of Ideas and Bonding with a Team

Sometimes the problem-solving process allows for an organization to communicate and work as a team as nothing else can do. It can become a bonding experience. I've been through some tough financial issues—we were even victims of an embezzlement once! However, the bond that experience created between our bank, our board, and our staff is a trust akin to family. I'm not saying that I'd love to go through that whole nightmare again, but it allowed for the creative exchange of ideas, the implementation of solutions, and solidified us as a team.

Problems Allow Leaders to Grow and Gain Wisdom

Experience is the only teacher that provides wisdom. Even good godly counsel doesn't always give us the firsthand knowledge we need to make good decisions. If you can, step emotionally away from a problem when you're in the middle of it and ask what the positive results can and will be. Make mental notes or even journal the experience so that your newfound wisdom will overflow into other difficult circumstances.

Problems Allow God to Be God

I wrote a song a few years ago called "God of Miracles." As my father lay dying of cancer, it was his favorite song to listen to. The line he liked best is "If I never had a need, I'd never see a miracle." And we did experience a miracle as he passed from life to life—no eternal death for a believer.

Problems—especially ones that seem to have no human solution—show God to be God. Think of the problems that Christ encountered that allowed miracles to be performed: if it weren't for hungry people, the five thousand would not have been fed; if not for the blind, they would not have been given sight; if not for the sick, they would not have been healed.

In fact, when questioned by the disciples as to whose sin caused a certain man's blindness, Jesus responded, "Neither this man nor his parents sinned . . . but this happened so that the work of God might be displayed in His life" (John 9:3).

When we acknowledge God's sovereign will, we recognize that there will be those occasions when He allows problems to come our way, so "that the work of God might be displayed" through His mighty hand of power, producing miraculous results. What a privilege to be allowed to see Him in action this way in our lives.

Can you look at a problem as a miraculous opportunity? Can you view a problem as a challenge to finding a creative solution? Can you accept problems as a vehicle for God's work to be displayed in your life? If you can, you will reap incredible benefits as you face head on your problems as positive impulses from God.

The Ten Commandments: The Most Effective Way to Prevent Problems

Finally, I want to leave you with ten familiar commandments that, if followed, will help you prevent problems from occurring in the first place and certainly guide you in dealing with any difficulties that do crop up.

Please allow me the liberty to give these familiar commandments a twenty-first-century spin that applies to women in their homes, schools, churches, offices, and leadership roles today. I guarantee that adherence to these prevention principles will help you avoid dealing with difficulties later on.

1. "You shall have no other gods before me" (Ex. 20:3).

Prevention Principle: You shall prioritize work, soccer practice, shopping, and time on the phone with your friends so that you spend quality time with God. He *must* be the most prevalent and important thing on your mind at all times.

2. "You shall not make for yourself an idol in the form of anything in heaven above or on the earth beneath or in the waters below" (Ex. 20:4).

Prevention Principle: You shall choose to worship God first rather than to sit and worship at the foot of the television set, surf the Web, or give your total devotion to another human being.

3. "You shall not misuse the name of the Lord your God, for the Lord will

not hold anyone guiltless who misuses his name" (Ex. 20:7).

Prevention Principle: You shall use God's name only with reverence and awe, praising Him for who He is.

4. "Remember the Sabbath day by keeping it holy" (Ex. 20:8).

Prevention Principle: Remember that God can heal our troubled souls and weary bodies only if we take time to rest in Him.

5. "Honor your father and your mother so that you may live long in the land the Lord your God is giving you" (Ex. 20:12).

Prevention Principle: You shall show respect and meet your duty of obligation to those who have sacrificed for you and invested in your future.

6. "You shall not murder" (Ex. 20:13).

Prevention Principle: You shall control your anger so that it does not lead to hurtful words or damaging actions.

7. "You shall not commit adultery" (Ex. 20:14).

Prevention Principle: Faithfulness will protect you from suffering undue emotional stress and sexually transmitted diseases. It also shall provide a role model of self-discipline, compromise, persistence, and compassion for those who will emulate you.

8. "You shall not steal" (Ex. 20:15).

Prevention Principle: You shall give credit to others for even their ideas and not steal any of their recognition.

9. "You shall not give false testimony against your neighbor" (Ex. 20:16).

Prevention Principle: You shall use words and ideas that serve only to edify and build up others.

10. "You shall not covet your neighbor's house . . . wife, . . . manservant or maidservant, his ox or donkey, or anything that belongs to your neighbor" (Ex. 20:17).

Prevention Principle: You shall rejoice when your neighbor moves into a house that is bigger than yours, drives a BMW, is married to a handsome spouse, has a cleaning lady or gardener, and takes trips to Europe each year. You shall not even be upset by the raise given to your peer who may not deserve it.

God gave us these commandments for our protection and provision. Think of how loving, kind, and fair our world of influence can be if we follow these wonderful principles of living. These ideas are not of this world and there are few who practice them. However, you and I can be instigators of change by implementing these Prevention Principles. We will reap the rewards of fewer problems, better communication, a stronger team, more loyalty and respect, a clear conscience, and God's favor.

Lord, help us as women who influence to follow the principles for successful living that You have outlined in Your Word. Give us discernment when it comes to preventing problems and wisdom in solving them. In everything, let us give You honor and glory! Amen.

Are You a Hands-on, a Hands-off or a "Hey, Mon, Who Cares?" Kinda Girl? Which Leadership Style Is Best for You?

Participatory management, servant leadership, the Scanlon plan. Perhaps you've heard some of these phrases thrown around and know that they somehow reflect something about a leadership philosophy. But you might not be totally clear about exactly what.

For this reason, I'd like to define several leadership models commonly discussed today and provide some biblical examples of the good, the bad, and the ungodly. Once you've sifted through the theory, you may see how one approach or elements of several can benefit you where you are right now—as a leader in your home or professional situation. Perhaps you will also see some possible pitfalls of adopting certain leadership philosophies.

I've ended this section with a discussion of servant leadership since it is the most Christlike model for us to follow. Servant leadership really embodies many of the best elements of each of the other philosophies.

Leader Qualifications

From God's perspective, what are leadership qualifications? To answer this question, let's focus in on the life of King David.

The scriptural account of David begins in 1 Samuel 16. The Prophet Samuel is sent by God to the home of Jesse to anoint the next king of Israel. Naturally, Samuel gravitates towards Eliab, Jesse's first-born son. However, Samuel immediately recognizes that this is *not* God's chosen.

In fact, he calls each of Jesse's sons to pass in front of him, seven in all. Samuel finally turns to Jesse and says, "Are these all the sons you have?" Like seven isn't enough? No, there was still the youngest, David, out tending the sheep. Probably the most unlikely of the clan to ever be considered for such a position as king, but Dad Jesse sent for him anyway.

When David comes into their presence, the Lord commands Samuel to "Rise and anoint him; he is the one" (v. 12).

Can you imagine the reaction from the seven brothers? "You've got to be kidding!" "This kid doesn't know anything but sheep herding!" "He's still wet behind the ears!" "Why would God choose our youngest brother and not one of us?"

The answer lies within verse 7: "Do not consider his appearance or his height. . . . The Lord does not look at the things man looks at. Man looks at the outward appearance, but the Lord looks at the heart."

What does it mean to be a leader after "God's own heart?" Look at Exodus 34:6 and let's discover the character qualities that God reveals about His own heart to Moses: He is

- Compassionate

- Gracious

- Slow to anger

- Abounding in love

- Faithful

- Forgiving

What this says is that we don't need a master's degree in business or marketing, twenty-five years of experience in the corporate arena, or a title that designates an authority position to have the heart of a leader. Effective leadership can and will overflow naturally from within our hearts if the heart is reflective of God's character.

Did you catch the other requirement? Saul was stripped of his leadership role by God because he did not keep His commandments. Samuel told him, "The Lord has sought out a man after his own heart and appointed him leader of his people, because you have not kept the Lord's command" (1 Sam. 13:14). When our priority is to develop godly character qualities and obey God's commands, we become equipped for leadership.

Let's continue examining the life of Saul as an example of one leadership style.

Authoritative Leadership

Authoritative leadership plants its roots in the philosophy that the boss is always right, has the prerogative to make any decision at any time without consultation or question, and is the final authority on most issues—even minor ones. Many who own their own businesses feel inclined to rule from this leadership style, and perhaps rightly so, since it is their money invested and they have the most to win or lose.

If there were a diagram or flow chart to describe this style of leadership, the leader would be at the top of the pyramid with the managers, workers, and customers below her, each dependent upon the leader for instruction.

The pitfall of true authoritative leadership is that the leader risks losing valuable input from workers who may bring helpful insight and wisdom. The other caution for this leader is that he or she quickly becomes bigger than the mission of the organization. Although it's important for people to "buy into" the leader, it's also important that the mission is the central focus, rather than pleasing or displeasing the boss.

Saul's disobedience to God, as revealed in 1 Samuel 13 and 15, exemplifies a leader who is unwilling to listen to not just godly counsel but *God Himself*! His reliance upon his own authority led to his demise as God's appointed king of Israel.

Saul's disobedience to God's will resulted in Samuel relaying this message from God: "You acted foolishly. . . . You have not kept the command the Lord your God gave you. . . . Now your kingdom will not endure" (1 Sam. 13:13-14).

There are elements of authoritative leadership that we can embrace; there certainly needs to be a place for the buck to stop and for final decisions to be made. However, there is a danger in relying solely upon self in setting the course. Most of us lack within ourselves the ability to make all the decisions correctly all by ourselves all of the time.

We do well to follow the advice of Jehoshaphat in 1 Kings 22:5: "First seek the counsel of the Lord," for "plans fail for lack of counsel, but with many advisers, they succeed" (Prov. 15:22).

Laissez Faire Leadership

While the laissez faire leadership style is less likely to be practiced by a business owner who has a vested interest in succeeding, a manager who does not take ownership in her own responsibility may fall into it. This leader places low value on relationships within the organization and provides little or no structure for people or self to work within. The result is often low productivity, no accountability, and lack of focus on goals.

Second Samuel 13 records the tragic story of David's firstborn son, Amnon. It seems that Amnon was more interested in satisfying personal lusts than in developing relationships with his father's valuable network, honing his fighting skills, and learning how to succeed his father as king. We would have expected the firstborn to be taking steps in being groomed for leadership. Instead, "Though first in line to succeed his father, Amnon never became a leader in Israel because of his lack of self-discipline. Manipulated by unwise counsel and driven by lust, Amnon raped his half sister and was murdered in retaliation by Absalom, Tamar's vengeful brother."[1]

This certainly is an extreme example of laissez faire leadership, but Amnon demonstrated what happens when there is no focus on personal or professional growth goals or accountability. Contrast his attitude with that of Solomon who eventually did succeed his father, David: "Solomon showed his love for the Lord by walking according to the statutes of his father David" (1 Kings 3:3). Because Solomon had a willingness to be mentored by David (1 Kings 2), he, not Amnon, was given the throne of Israel.

Delegative Leadership

Delegative leadership displays trust in people and gives them freedom of latitude in getting the job done. This style, however, risks being ineffective by trying to avoid conflict. When there is nowhere for the buck to stop, it is often difficult to keep workers accountable for their actions. Also, it often assigns responsibility, but not authority. The positive outcome of delegative leadership is that the leader has learned to let go of tasks and assign them to others who are trustworthy.

The leadership life of Moses is filled with examples of delegative leadership that often proved successful and sometimes failed.

Exodus 18 is rich in leadership lessons from the perspective of Moses' father-in-law, Jethro. Jethro was a good listener, an intuitive onlooker, and an obedient servant of God. As he observed Moses wearing himself out by trying to settle disputes among the Children of Israel, he offered this wise observation: "The work is too heavy for you; you cannot handle it alone" (v. 18). "Select capable men from all the people—men who fear God, trustworthy men who hate dishonest gain—and appoint them as officials over thousands, hundreds, fifties and tens. Have them serve as judges for the people at all times, but have them bring every difficult case to you. . . . That will make your load lighter, because they will share it with you" (vv. 21-22). Sharing the load is what delegative leadership is all about.

What incredible advice to us today. However, the key to its success is in choosing those who are totally committed and qualified to be delegated to. Unfortunately for Moses, a few chapters later, he delegates responsibility to his brother, Aaron, to run things while Moses is meeting with God on Mt. Sinai.

Aaron many times demonstrates that he does not possess the same leadership qualities as does Moses; he just doesn't have the same trust in God that Moses displays and it certainly hurts him and the people he is supposed to be leading.

Exodus 32 describes the familiar scene where Aaron not only gives in to the people's grumbling and allows them to construct a golden calf to worship, but he actually takes an active part in collecting the rings and forming the idol. Then, he has the audacity to lie about it when confronted by Moses! "They gave me the gold, and I threw it into the fire, and out came this calf!" (v. 24). No wonder Moses' anger was so great that he threw down and smashed the tablets God had given him (v. 19). Ironically, the first commandment God had written on those tablets was "You shall have no other gods before me" (Ex. 20:3).

Collaborative Leadership

Collaborative leadership provides a high level of emotional support and involvement from the leader. It is true team management at work where direction is a collaborative effort; each member of the team providing guidance. Its success relies upon strong and genuine relationships within the team. Any power plays among the workers can foil its effectiveness, and either a designated leader must take the reigns and give direction, or the group must rally to expel the power seeker.

Acts 1 begins at the point where Jesus is taken up into heaven and the remaining eleven disciples are left to decide where to go from there. They have been given the Great Commission by Jesus to "be my witnesses in Jerusalem, and in all Judea and Samaria, and to the ends of the earth" (v. 8).

The disciples demonstrate beautifully the concept of collaborative leadership. Together they discuss and agree upon a plan that will fill the disciple vacancy left by Judas and come up with a strategy to fulfill their mandate. Although Peter is the one who stands up and states the obvious, we don't get the impression that any decision was made without open discussion and total agreement. And "They all joined together constantly in prayer" (v. 14). Together they acknowledged their true authority—God—and were willing to submit to that will. How precious the bond must have been between these friends of Jesus. They had shared in His ministry, death, resurrection, and ascension, and now were in agreement as to how to proceed in the continuing ministry.

The Scanlon Plan

Closely aligned to collaborative leadership is the Scanlon plan.[2] This leadership philosophy includes workers in the financial benefits made from their contributions—stock options, if you will. In effect, they are also owners of the corporation with a vested monetary interest in seeing it succeed.

As the parable of the talents illustrates in Matthew 25, when we are good stewards of God's resources, we see a return on our investments and have the opportunity to be given even more.

Although this parable was told by Jesus to describe His second coming, it demonstrates in degree the philosophy of the Scanlon plan. The master embarks on a journey and gives a unit of money, or talents, to each of three servants. To the most capable, he gives five talents; to the next capable, two; and to another just one talent.

The first two servants, seeing opportunity to please the master, promote his business, and personally enjoy financial gain, wisely invest their talents. They view this as an opportunity to take ownership. The result is that they double their investments. The third servant, however, didn't even invest the money in a bank where it would make interest, but just buried it.

When the master returns, he is so pleased with the first two servants—pleased for himself and the gain for his household, and pleased that they could also enjoy financial increase. However, the servant that buried the one talent he was given was punished severely. Not only was he a poor steward of the master's gift, but he forfeited his own financial reward as well.

The first two servants, in effect, became joint owners of the master's fortune because of the personal ownership they undertook in investing their talents. Although a money term in the New Testament, we now refer to gifts as talents. Are you and I investing them so as to see maximum return in the kingdom of God?

Participatory Leadership

Also closely aligned with collaborative leadership, participatory leadership aligns the leader alongside her managers, workers, customers, and expert consultants. She understands and sees the vision and sets broad guidelines, then allows her workers to set the agenda for attaining goals.

She understands that there are times when the buck stops with her and that she must make an executive decision. However, she tries her best to help everyone buy into the decision by listening and discussing the major issues. She doesn't micromanage and knows how to delegate. She not only gives responsibility, but empowers her people by giving them the authority to make the decisions they need to for their portion to run smoothly.

The prophetess Deborah as described in Judges 4 so beautifully illustrates participatory leadership.

Deborah receives the word from God that they are to attack Sisera, the commander of the Canaanite army who had oppressed Israel for twenty years. When she lays out the plan of attack for Barak, the commander of the Israelite army, his fear overtakes him and he begs Deborah to accompany him.

She never hesitates to support him in this effort and comes alongside him in the attack. How easy it would have been for her to say, "That's your job! I'm gonna sit right here under my Palm of Deborah where I always hold court, and send you on your way without listening to your fears or concerns."

Instead, she allows for give and take so that Barak can buy into the idea and truly listens to his fears and concerns. She is not afraid to allow others to participate in the discussion or to involve herself as her people desire. Effective leaders never ask their people to do what they are not willing to do.

Situational Leadership

Situational leadership employs a variety of leadership styles, depending upon the situation and the level of development of the people involved. A fairly inexperienced staff would seek the guidance, direction, and decisions based on the authoritative leadership style. However, a highly experienced and capable staff could be given full collaborative leadership, complete with delegation and decision-making rights.

Management expert Kenneth Blanchard's premise is that workers fall into one of four categories that are always in a process of evolution. There is the enthusiastic beginner (excited but with little knowledge), the disillusioned learner (learning a task that is tougher than she thought), the capable but cautious performer (knows what to do but lacks confidence), and the self-reliant achiever (has all the necessary skills, including motivation and confidence).[3]

Good leadership will continuously train and encourage growth from one category to another. Therefore, leadership methodology will vary, and thus is situational, depending upon where the workers fall in these categories.

When Christ called together His ragtag team of disciples in Luke 6:12-16, they were by no means ready to serve or lead. And each possessed his own unique personality and experiential credentials. Therefore the playing ground was not equal for all who were called.

Scripture records how Jesus continually fluctuated His leadership style to comply with their needs and the situations they were facing until one day, when He was no longer there, they were fully equipped to serve (Acts 2).

Notice how Jesus throughout the Gospels leads as a role model in performing miracles, casting out demons, and teaching through parables. In each situation, He sheds just a little more light upon who He is and how the disciples will eventually lead. He asks questions, tells stories, and even rebukes at times . . . all in conformance with situational leadership.

Servant Leadership

Ultimately, even though Christ exemplified situational leadership, His most outstanding leadership model was that of servant leadership. In Matthew 20:28 He tells us that He "did not come to be served, but to serve, and to give his life as a ransom for many."

Max DePree says that "Leaders belong to their followers . . . and should refer to (them) as 'the people I serve.'"[4]

Bob Briner echoes the same thought: "The way to succeed is to put others first."[5] Matthew 23:11 records Jesus affirming this by saying: "The greatest among you will be your servant."

So how do we become servant leaders without feeling as if we are doormats?

James O'Toole answers this way: "The leader is the 'servant' of his (or her) followers in that he/she removes the obstacles that prevent them from doing their jobs. In short, the true leader enables his or her followers to realize their full potential."[6]

Did you get that? Servant leaders see the potential in others and do everything possible to help them reach up to their potentials. When you and I reach up to our leadership potentials, we fulfill Christ's purpose for us. As our servant leader, His will is that we develop the gifts and talents that He has given to us so that we are obedient to Him and fit for service in His kingdom. In turn, we are expected to influence and mentor others in the same way.

So, what character qualities comprise servant leadership and does this philosophy have any validity for us today? Let's go to the Scriptures to discover how Jesus served His followers. As we study His servant leadership model, my prayer is that you and I, then, will slowly begin to integrate these techniques into our own leadership style. Just as Solomon's masterpiece of a temple was not built in a day, so it is a long process for us to develop such lofty abilities. In fact, let me encourage you by reminding you that even Jesus was given thirty years of preparation before He began His earthly ministry—and He was the Son of God! Let's look at why people followed Him and what He offered them.

Jesus Taught with Authority

Mark 1:22 records, "The people were amazed at his teaching, because he taught them as one who had authority, not as the teachers of the law."

Servant leadership requires extensive knowledge and exhaustive preparation that earns respect for the leader's authority. Are there areas where you and I need to improve our expertise? Would some further study or life experience add to the richness of our example and teaching?

In most leadership models, it is evident that the best leaders are also teachers. How can you and I become better equipped to train, encourage, and mentor those in our sphere of influence?

Jesus Took Care of People

Revisit Matthew 8:14-15. Each miracle of Jesus displayed His incredible concern for others, but one such example stands out to us as we look at Jesus as the servant to His disciples, committed to caring for their needs.

Apparently Peter's mother-in-law was lying in bed with a fever when Jesus arrived there. We can just imagine the concern Peter's wife and circle of friends must have had for her health. We don't get the impression that anyone told Jesus about her illness; He just walks into the house, takes her hand, and the fever leaves her. Think of the elation she must have felt to be well enough to witness all of the miracles that Jesus would perform later that evening. And think of the privilege it was for her to be able to serve Him in return.

John's account of Jesus' miracles ends by saying, "Jesus did many other things as well. If every one of them were written down, I suppose that even the whole world would not have room for the books that would be written" (John 21:25). However, with all of the deeds that Jesus performed, His priority concern was for the heart condition of His followers. In Matthew's account of the healing of the paralytic, (9:1-8), before healing the man, Jesus said, "Take heart, son; your sins are forgiven." Servant leadership displays a concern for people's souls as well as their earthly needs. Servant leadership demonstrates concern through personal involvement.

Jesus Demonstrated Compassion Through Touch

"Filled with compassion, Jesus reached out his hand and touched the man" (Mark 1:41). "Then he touched their eyes and . . . their sight was restored" (Matt. 9:29-30). "But when he [Peter] saw the wind, he was afraid and, beginning to sink, cried out, 'Lord, save me!' Immediately Jesus reached out his hand and caught him." (Matt. 14:30-31).

Servant leadership involves compassion strong enough to reach out and touch those around us who are in need of encouragement. Remember, people need at least twelve touches per day to feel significant.

Max DePree calls this the "language of touch." "Only through touch are plans and agendas and visions made real. Only through action can a language—any language—ramify itself in our world. . . . We have to begin to think more carefully about renewing the ministry or language of touch in our communities."[7] Servant leadership touches others with compassion.

Jesus Was Not Arrogant

John the Baptist declared, "But after me will come one who is more powerful than I, whose sandals I am not fit to carry" (Matt. 3:11). Yet in John 13:5, displaying the most humble act of servanthood, Jesus washed the feet of His disciples, which is a menial task usually assigned to the lowliest of servants. In verse 15 He says, "I have set you an example that you should do as I have done for you."

Having been a part of the Christian music industry for many years, I have seen a variety of Christian artists come and go. In God's economy, none is greater than another, yet there are some who will quickly fall along the wayside as arrogance destroys them. They might as well have "It's all about me!" tattooed on their foreheads, because "It's all about my Lord" is the furthest thing from their minds.

Contrast this to the servant leadership model that Dr. Woody Voller lived out before me when I was a student at Spring Arbor College. During a fundraiser where we hosted an auction, a man who had purchased a dresser grabbed the first blue-jeaned male he saw and enlisted his help in hoisting the new piece of furniture into the back of his pickup truck. As if this wasn't enough, the purchaser also asked the man to ride with him to his home and help him unload it, which he cheerfully agreed to.

Thinking that this bulky, rough-sawn guy was a part of the janitorial staff, the gentleman began conversation by asking just what he did for the college. When Dr. Voller revealed that he was the president, the man just about swerved into the ditch! Dr. Voller's lack of arrogance paid off when the embarrassed individual soon after made a sizable contribution to the college!

Jesus Demonstrated Humbleness Through Sacrifice

Jesus was willing to make sacrifices—even unto death on a cross. Although servant leadership usually does not require that we literally give our lives for the cause we represent, it certainly will require significant sacrifices.

John Maxwell calls this the "cost of leadership." He says, "As you rise in leadership, responsibilities increase and rights decrease. . . . You've got to give up to go up."[8] Sacrifice takes many forms including time away from enjoyable activities or family and demonstrating financial restraint. For four years now I have forfeited taking a salary from the TimeOut for Women! organization in hopes that I can adequately provide for the paid workers and help advance the ministry. I have never had one moment of regret since God continues to bless my life with opportunity to minister and an inner peace that comes from being obedient. He has always taken care of my needs so that I can take care of the needs of those who depend upon me. I *love* the element of servant sacrifice for the benefit of bringing others to know Christ!

The leader is in place to serve, not to be served. Leaders are to function for the benefit of the people, not the people for the benefit of the leader. "Leaders don't inflict pain; they bear pain."[9] Servant leadership joyfully commits acts of sacrifice for the benefit of the followers.

Jesus Gave Credit Where Credit Was Due

If I were in Jesus' shoes and ministering with thousands of people following me, it would have been *so* tempting to say, "Yes, look what I just did! Aren't I wonderful?" However, Jesus gave all of the credit to His Father: "I do nothing on my own but speak just what the Father has taught me. The one who sent me is with me; he has not left me alone, for I always do what pleases him" (John 8:28-29).

When Jesus observed what we now term the story of the widow's mite, he gave this woman credit for faithfulness: "He also saw a poor widow put in two very small copper coins. 'I tell you the truth,' he said, 'this poor widow has put in more than all the others. All these people gave their gifts out of their wealth; but she out of her poverty put in all she had to live on'" (Luke 21:2-4).

Other times when healing the sick, Jesus would commend them by saying, "Your faith has made you well" (Luke 17:19). Servant leaders are willing to praise, commend, and give credit where credit is due.

Jesus Granted Authority

Jesus not only assigned responsibility, but granted authority to fulfill that responsibility.

Nothing is more frustrating than being given a job to do and not the tools to complete it successfully. It would be like my asking you to stand at the basketball free throw line to make a basket and handcuffing your hands behind your back.

Jesus, the master teacher and servant leader, trained His followers to walk in His footsteps, then delegated to them the authority to act on His behalf. Matthew 10:1 records that "He called his twelve disciples to him and gave them authority to drive out evil spirits and to heal every disease and sickness."

Later, in Acts 1, He continues to equip them for their mandate by providing them with the gift of the Holy Spirit. Acts 1:8: "But you will receive power when the Holy Spirit comes on you." Servant leaders are willing to empower their followers to act on their behalf.

Jesus Demonstrated Humility

Jesus humbled himself to fulfill His purpose for the greater good: "I am not seeking glory for myself" (John 8:50). In Matthew 23:12, Christ reveals the benefits of humbleness: "Whoever humbles himself will be exalted."

Though Heavenly King and Ruler of all, Jesus humbled Himself to be born a peasant baby with the sole (or perhaps soul) purpose to give that life for us. He said, "Now my heart is troubled, and what shall I say? 'Father, save me from this hour'? No, it was for this very reason I came to this hour. Father, glorify your name!" (John 12:27-28).

Something supernatural happened to the hotheaded Peter from the time Christ called him until he wrote his letters. There is certainly hope for you and me. Peter says, "Clothe yourselves with humility toward one another, because, 'God opposes the proud but gives grace to the humble.' Humble yourselves, therefore, under God's mighty hand, that he may lift you up in due time" (1 Peter 5:5-6).

God should decide if and when we should be "lifted up" to receive recognition. Whether we ever "receive our due" in this life is inconsequential; what only matters is whether we are fit to be "lifted up" with Christ and ascend with Him to the place He has prepared for us.

Servant leadership requires that humility takes precedence over recognition.

Are You Up for Servant Service as You Lead?

As these examples have shown, Jesus implemented an ongoing training program for the continuous improvement and growth of His disciples. In Matthew 13:36 the disciples come to Jesus and say, "Explain to us the parable." From then on, the exchange between Christ and the disciples is one of His teaching, their asking questions, and Jesus testing them with questions to see if they really "got it." He taught and prepared them for leadership right up until His death. Servant leadership mentors others so that they can be servant leaders.

The greatest leaders are those who see potential in others and are willing to invest their lives into producing offspring. This takes a person who is willing to put ego and pride on a back burner so that the recognition goes to others in the organization.

Leadership is not control and domination of others. "It is a choice opportunity to guide, encourage, and help others to be productive and successful. It is a spiritual ministry."[10]

"As for the best leaders, the people do not notice their existence. The next best, the people honor and praise. The next, the people fear; and the next, the people hate. . . . When the best leader's work is done the people say, 'We did it ourselves!'"[11]

"In the kingdom of God, the way up is down. Jesus overturned contemporary notions of power and replaced them with the paradox of servant leadership. In a sense He was saying, 'It doesn't matter who has the title. Look for the one with the servant's heart, and there you've found your leader.' As in all other areas, He Himself is the perfect example."[12]

Perhaps leaders are born, but they can also be made. Do you have the heart of a servant? Even more importantly, are you, like David, a person "after God's own heart"? Do you possess a vision for what you know will make this world a better place? Do you have an idea for a ministry or business concept that will fulfill a life's dream you've been carrying in your heart?

If so, it's time to take the intangible and make it tangible. It's time to put wings to your ideas and let them fly. It's time to make your dream a reality. "But those who hope in the Lord will renew their strength. They will soar on wings like eagles; they will run and not grow weary, they will walk and not be faint" (Isa. 40:31).

Lord, Jesus, it is such a privilege to serve You. We now ask for the privilege to serve others in a way that will glorify You. Plant within us that servant's heart, then give us the desire of our heart that is intended to fulfill Your purpose. Give us a heart after Your own heart! Surface our innermost dreams and mesh them with the natural talent You have created within us. Grant us the passion now to take definite action in making these dreams come true. Let Your dream begin within us! Amen.

Putting It All Together:
Let the Dream Begin!

So you now have a plethora of valuable information to guide and direct you as your abilities in leadership grow. What are you going to do with it all? Well, since "faith without deeds is dead" (James 2:26), I want to encourage you to act upon your dream—TODAY!

No one ever just stumbles upon success or achievement; no one ever fulfills a dream by just thinking about it. Success is the result of deliberate planning and takes place when preparation meets opportunity. And remember that the point of attaining goals is so that you can continually reach to live up to your God-given potential. For this reason, I want to walk you through a strategy that will assure you of attaining your goals, of fulfilling your dreams—of living up to your potential. It's called Ponder, Plan, Proceed.

Ponder

Everything begins with an idea. An idea can be born only if we take the time to think, to meditate, to pray, and yes, to dream. I've heard of one major U.S. corporation that requires its high level executives to spend at least one hour per week on the top floor of its corporate headquarters, lying on a waterbed, gazing out the skylight daydreaming!

Think of the wisdom in this. Have you ever struggled with an issue all day, only to fall into bed exhausted, then startled awake in the middle of the night with the solution? Or, upon awakening in the stillness of the morning, as the sun is just creeping along the horizon, have you heard a few words in your mind with a melody to hum with it? Do you remember as a student studying for an exam the last thing at night, sleeping on the information, and finding that you remembered most of it the next day for the test?

There is something amazing, perhaps miraculous, about the human mind. When we take away distracting noises and stimulating visuals, our thoughts have an opportunity to wander, often leading us exactly where our conscious attempts could not.

So take time to Ponder. Think *big* and think *often*. Let your imagination go wild with possibilities. *Dream!*

Let me warn you: do *not* let your ideas evaporate into thin air. Remember the section on brainstorming for writing and speaking? Make your ideas *real* by writing them down. Write down any dream, goal, or destination that comes to your mind, even if it seems a little crazy: a safari in Africa, a year studying in Paris, writing a book, playing the guitar, starting a business, finishing your degree—your potentials and possibilities are *endless!* What is *in* your heart that you want to live *out* in a dream?

You may have swallowed a certain desire for many years, thinking that it would never happen to you. Well, sister, it is time for you to take steps to *make* it happen. And it all begins with a dream. Ponder as long as you need to and be sure to write down everything and anything you would like to set as a goal to accomplish.

Plan

In 1952, a respected university conducted a study of its graduates. The survey revealed that only 3 percent of those who graduated that year wrote down a clear list of goals. Ten years later, a follow-up study revealed that exactly 3 percent of that graduating class had accomplished more financially than the remaining 97 percent. It came as no surprise that those 3 percent were the same graduates who had written down their goals.[1] An unwritten goal is merely a wish. A written goal will likely become a reality.

Achievement begins with clear, attainable goals. So what makes a goal a goal? One expert put it this way: *A goal is a dream with a deadline.* I've learned to put into practice a helpful technique that has assisted me in book writing, music production, and event coordination: *begin with the end in mind.*

When I was asked to write a song for a college graduation ceremony, the first thing I did was to picture myself standing on the stage in the arena singing to the five hundred graduates who would sit directly before me and the five thousand spectators sitting around the circumference of the "bowl." I imagined the heartwarming scenario of the single mom who took night classes for three years to complete her degree. Her mom, sister, and four-year-old son are sitting off to the side with tears just streaming down their cheeks as she crosses the stage to receive her diploma.

I thought of the businessman who up to this time had been denied promotions because he did not possess a business degree. He walks up to the college president, shakes hands, and the college president ceremoniously moves the tassel on his mortarboard from one side to the other. His wife and teenaged daughter stand and applaud.

I saw the grandma and grandpa who had sacrificed taking trips, buying a bigger house, and getting a newer car to put their grandson through college. Now at twenty-two, tall and gangly, he shyly walks up the steps as his name is called. Grandma clutches her handkerchief to her breast as Grandpa lovingly places his arms around her shoulders.

My inspiration for the song came from seeing, touching, and feeling the *end*. What did I want them to feel when I sang this song? What message—their very last one from college—did I want them to carry with them? All teary-eyed from this picture painted in my mind, the words just tumbled out:

> The time has come to leave this place
> And let the dream begin
> Let the spark become the flame
> That lights a fire within
>
> The time has come to be set free
> To soar the endless sky
> Following your heartfelt dreams
> Spread your wings and fly!
>
> It's time to let the dream begin
> Dawning with each bright tomorrow
> Guided by God's truth to follow
> Light that shows the way
>
> It's time to let the dream begin
> Burning with your heart's desire
> Run the race and never tire
> The dream begins today!
>
> And just remember as you go
> You are never alone!
> Spread your wings and fly
> Let the dream begin—
> Reach for the sky![2]

So, dear sister, it is time for you to reach for the sky. Together we are going to decide on an attainable goal and then plan the sequence of short-term deadlines so you can let your dream begin. Let's start by thinking about what dream you want to be fulfilled. (Remember that it must be realistic, attainable, and measurable.)

List the necessary steps involved that will lead to the accomplishment of your dream. List these in chronological order.

Research and determine any costs involved. Is the dream still realistic? Are there short-term goals (saving money, becoming certified, putting in more time, taking out a loan, etc.) that you must accomplish before you can actually let the dream begin?

Determine a timeline. Using your day planner, write out a specific time plan for accomplishing each smaller goal necessary to attain the greater goal. This will keep you from procrastinating, will keep a written goal before you at all times, and will be integrated into your regular routine.

Let's illustrate this procedure by using the scenario of going back to college and finishing your degree. Your dream: to complete your college degree in social work so you can help inner-city kids.

The steps involved might include:

Making an appointment in your calendar of when you plan to call the college.

On that date, call the registrar or admissions counselor and make an appointment to meet. Also coordinate an appointment with financial aid for the same day.

Place the appointments on your calendar.

Meet with the college staff on that day to determine how many classes you need to graduate and what type of financial aid is available.

Organize all of the paperwork (applications, financial aid requests, etc.), placing on your calendar when each is due and where it should be sent.

Decide how many classes you can take per term depending upon cost, time, and other commitments.

Write out the tentative course schedule for each term that will eventually earn you your degree. As each term begins, write in your day planner the class meeting times (if you meet Mondays and Wednesdays from 6 to 9 P.M., block out that time each week for the length of the term. Also, block out time for study and research before the calendar fills up.)

Based upon this plan, you should be able to set a date for your graduation party!

You get the idea. Every goal can be accomplished through the attainment of incremental goals along the way. A good rule of thumb is this: Set goals in stone; plans in sand. In other words, if your goal is your final destination on the road map, remember that you can get there by taking a variety of roads. One course may offer too many detours and delays, so try another plan. But always keep your goal as the bulls-eye you aim your arrow at!

And remember to aim high! As one philosopher put it, "Aim at the sun and you may not reach it, but your arrow will fly far higher than if aimed at an object on a level with yourself."

Proceed

Now that you've got a plan for attaining your goals and dreams, it's time to proceed. It's time to hit the road!

Hyrum Smith, author of *The 10 Natural Laws of Successful Time and Life Management*, paints a challenging picture of what it means to attain a goal: "A goal is a planned conflict with the status quo."[3] Setting and attaining goals that let your dream begin may force you to leave your comfort zone and explore new frontiers. It may involve deliberately creating conflict in your routine and expectations. Go for it! Here are some ways that you can meet the challenge:

Be Persistent

Many times the difference between success and failure is persistence. How many business owners give up too soon? How many, when the going gets tough, throw up their hands in surrender and say, "I give up" ? And where does it get them? Back to nowhere—the place they came from.

When I think of the value of persistence, the life of Abraham Lincoln always comes to mind. Look at the failures he endured before finally becoming President.

> In 1832 he not only lost his job, but was defeated for the legislature. In 1833, he failed in business. In 1836 he suffered a nervous breakdown. In 1838 he was defeated for speaker. In 1843 he was defeated for Congress. In 1848 he lost the nomination bid for Congress. In 1854 he was defeated for the Senate. In 1856 he lost the nomination for Vice President. In 1858 he was again defeated for the Senate. Then finally, in 1860 he was elected President.[4]

What kept Lincoln going through all of these defeats? My conclusion is two things: his faith that he was following the will of God and his overriding vision for what America could and should be. Quitting takes no guts and no courage. Persistence is praiseworthy and courageous.

Look at the Benefits of Obstacles

I would venture to say that most of Lincoln's equipping and preparation process for the White House originated in the lessons he learned from his opposition, setbacks, and obstacles. He was a stronger, more decisive, and confident leader because of them. Every moving object experiences resistance. However, we can allow setbacks to propel us forward.

"When one door closes, another opens; but we often look so long and regretfully upon the closed door that we do not see the one which has opened for us."[5] Obstacles often change our direction, but they do not need to deter us from our destination.

Proverbs 27:17 reminds us that "As iron sharpens iron, so one man sharpens another." Obstacles can defeat us, or they can sharpen us. They can tempt us to quit, or they can propel us to continue. If we are wise, we will view them as valuable lessons that will benefit us as we accomplish each incremental goal to fulfilling the dream.

An old proverb reminds us that a diamond cannot be polished without friction, nor the [wo]man perfected without trials.

Stay Focused

If you clearly see your vision and know in your heart that you are proceeding within the will of God, you must keep your eyes focused on the goal. Proverbs 4:25, 27 instructs, "Let your eyes look straight ahead, fix your gaze directly before you. . . . Do not swerve to the right or the left." Hebrews 12:2-3: "Let us fix our eyes on Jesus, the author and perfecter of our faith. . . . Consider him who endured such opposition from sinful men, so that you will not grow weary and lose heart."

Our success depends upon who our focus is upon and our ability to concentrate on His purposes for us without being distracted.

Four-time Olympic medalist Madeline Manning Mims, inspired of God, sent me this message shortly after the new millennium began. She gave me permission to share it with you because she knows that focus is one of the characteristics necessary in a champion.

Even when My promises come true,
Focus on Me and not on you.
And even when calamities come your way,
Stay steadfast, unmovable in the fray.
When desperate times come to pull you down,
Look up for your help, keep your feet on the ground.

I will be moving in ways anew,
Fresh anointing for these times will fill you.
My power and might I will demonstrate;
I will come quickly to those who wait.
My wondrous works will abundantly abound.
I lift up the bowed head and bring the wicked down.

Nurture yourself in the love that is yours.
All that was shut is NOW an open door.
I will stand in the midst of every storm,
As you lean and depend on the everlasting arm.
Focus your eyes on the One who is the Head.
Be secured in His love and you won't be misled.

Humble yourself before My strong hand,
For I AM the Rock upon which you stand.
Turn not to the left nor the right, just follow where I lead.
My prayers go forth, on your behalf I intercede.
Your time is NOW, this is quite clear.
Abide in My Presence to find Me near.

And when the morning of day doth dawn,
Rest in the Rock you've leaned upon.
I come to reward your faithfulness,
For every heartache, for every test.
Looking through the eyes of faith you'll see.
When they see you, they will see Me.

So focus on Me, your life is in My hand.
You will not fall when in Christ you stand.
Your time is NOW, the world will know,
My grace and love I will bestow.
Mount up to prevail whatever the odds.
I NOW will show the world, that I AM the Only God![6]

Ask God to Guide Your Steps

"Delight yourself in the Lord and he will give you the desires of your heart" (Ps. 37:4). I don't know how you interpret this verse, but one day it occurred to me that it is *God* who places within us the desires of our hearts.

You may be a stay-at-home mom who quit college to get married and begin a family. The kids are now all in school and you feel that you have potential you're not living up to because you never finished your degree.

You may hold a position at a company where you feel your talents are underused and your abilities misunderstood. Deep in your heart is a tugging to move on to something more challenging and rewarding.

Perhaps you're just entering the "golden years" with children out of the nest, hubby still involved in his work, and you wonder if there is something more you should be contributing that would help others and give your life a greater purpose.

Maybe you're a single mom trapped in the relentless routine of work, meals, homework, and cleaning, but you know that you possess God-given talents that are not being honed.

No matter where you are positioned on the map of your life journey, let me encourage you to just STOP! Now, look in every direction to see where you are and what is surrounding you. Are you moving in a direction that fulfills your dreams and potential? Do you have a final goal as your destination on that map? Or are you like the little Boy Scout who got lost in the woods and after hours of walking discovered that he was just going in a big circle . . . getting nowhere fast?

If you feel that your life has no direction or purpose at this time, let me dispel that notion. It is a trick of Satan. God has gifted you with talents and He will bless you to see them fulfilled. You must seek Him and surrender your will to Him. So, let's take a moment and pray together that God will reveal Himself to you in a mighty way and make clear what your purpose is in the kingdom of God:

Dear Father, please clear away all the noise and distraction in the world of my dear sister at this time. Lord, help her to focus on You now. Envelop her with Your arms of love and understanding and help her feel Your compassion and tenderness. Then, Lord, overflow within her heart those things that You desire for her and make them her desires also. Show her opportunities in her life and how she can use her talents to glorify You. Reveal to her the next destination on her life journey map, and help her to take her first step on this new course.

Now, sweet sister, pray this prayer with me:

Lord, give me the desire of my heart and make my plans succeed. As I plan my course, determine my steps. I commit everything to You, Lord, knowing that through You my plans will succeed.[7]

A Pebble in the Pond:
The Ripple Effect

Mining the Pebble: Discovering Your Raw Potential

L et me close by retelling a tale known as "Acres of Diamonds." The original was told to Dr. Russell H. Conwell by his Turkish guide on the Tigris River in the 1800s.

The story goes that Ali Hafed was a very wealthy and contented man. He was contented because he was wealthy and wealthy because he was contented.

One day a Buddhist priest approached him, describing for him how diamonds were created from the hand of the Almighty as He swirled his finger in the fog until it became a solid ball of fire. He cast the fire out into the universe until its force careened over the crust of the earth digging out valleys and raising up mountains.

The priest maintained that from this fiery sphere the part that cooled quickly became granite; less quickly copper, less quickly silver, less quickly gold, and, after gold, diamonds were made.

Then the priest said, "A diamond is a congealed drop of sunlight. A diamond the size of my thumb could purchase a country and a diamond mine could place your children upon thrones."

Ali Hafed went to bed that night a poor man. Not because he had less wealth than before, but because he was discontented because he feared he was poor.

So, Ali Hafed set off to find happiness. He journeyed to discover the thing that would bring him wealth and contentment. He searched for diamonds in the Mountains of the Moon in Kenya, scoured Palestine, wandered through Europe, and finally, in filthy rags, money exhausted, Ali Hafed threw himself into a great tidal wave on the shores of Barcelona, Spain.

In the meantime, his successor, while watering his camel on Ali Hafed's farm, noticed a curious sparkle of light emanating from the sand. Seeing the stone, the priest excitedly exclaimed, "Has Ali returned? This must be the diamond he discovered and brought back with him!"

The successor just shook his head. Ali would never return. The priest and the successor began stirring around the sand to discover more and more beautiful and valuable gems.

"Thus," the guide told Conwell, "was discovered the diamond mine of Golconda, the most magnificent diamond mine in all the history of mankind."

Had Ali Hafed just remained at home, he would have discovered in his own backyard acres of diamonds.[1]

You must begin where you are with what you have. I am convinced that each of you possesses a wealth of diamonds—perhaps rough and uncut right now—but the wealth lies within you. You must recognize that God has given you talents that He considers of great value in His kingdom. He expects you to discover these gifts and know that He has a purpose and plan for the use of these gifts.

Cutting the Pebble: Allowing God to Equip You for Service

Diamonds in the rough are not readily recognized. Only the eye of the expert can see the potential beauty that lies within. "In its natural state, a diamond's beauty is generally well concealed. What makes it beautiful is the cut of the diamond—for it is the cut that unlocks the brilliance and fire of the diamond and lets it shine. . . . Only when precisely calculated planes and angles are used does the stone attain its greatest possible beauty. Needless to say, the cutting of a diamond requires great skill."[2]

The sharpening of our leadership qualities, much like the diamond, requires the same type of cutting and refining process. Our polishing effort requires precisely calculated plans and strategies. Our brilliance and fire can be unlocked if we are willing to submit ourselves to the skill of the Master Gem Cutter, Jesus Christ. "Commit your way to the Lord; trust in him and he will do this: He will make your righteousness shine like the dawn, the justice of your cause like the noonday sun" (Ps. 37:5-6).

In His hands, we become the clay that is fashioned by the Potter. In His hands, we are the seed that is planted with the purpose of bearing good fruits. In His hands, we are the diamond whose value is determined by how precise and deep the cuts of the Gem Cutter are. Our righteous Holy Father wants to take our lives and polish them so that His glory will shine before all people. He beckons us to submit to His equipping process so that we are poised to cast our pebble, allowing each ripple to touch the lives of those around us.

Casting the Pebble: Your Ripple Effect

If our deeds can be likened to a pebble, then the pond certainly should be likened to a vast array of people, pooled together to make up a pond unique to each of us. When we cast our pebble into that pond, what type of ripples will we see touch one life then another and another?

My husband and I met while he was working for the college that I was attending. At that time, he responded to a man, Dave Gines, who truly understood that his role was to train and mentor those he served. Many of his new, inexperienced employees were recent college graduates who quickly learned that their college degree was just a small part of building credentials to lead.

Through his patience, example, and wisdom, Dave's pebble has had an incredible ripple effect upon those who worked alongside of him. Three men who began their leadership journey with him in the early 1970s are Dr. David Gyerston, who has enjoyed presidencies at Regent University, Asbury College, and now Taylor University; Dr. Chuck Webb, who is currently the vice president for development at Michigan State University; and my husband, Paul Baker, who is vice president for advancement at Davenport University.

Frankly, if you could have seen this ragtag team then—a farm boy from Wisconsin, an orphan from Canada, and a poorer-than-the-church-mouse preacher's kid—you would never have dreamed that these uncut diamonds possessed the raw potential to shine this brilliantly. Now, each of them is affecting a sphere of influence as they lead in their own circle of responsibility. Although my husband's staff has never met Dave Gines, the pebble that Dave cast into Paul's life continues to expand and touch more and more uncut diamonds.

What raw potential do you have that needs cutting and polishing? It's time to Ponder, Plan, and Proceed with a strategy that will allow your talents to shine. Do you see unmined treasure in those around you? Then it's time to cast your pebble into the pond.

Fully equipped, the ripples we send into the world will spread out before us in ever concentric circles, the ultimate impact known only to God.

Endnotes

Introduction

1. Rowland. Source unknown.

Chapter One

1. Merrill Douglas, *Success Secrets* (Rapid City, S. Dak.: Honor Books, 1984) 107.

Chapter Two

1. Max Depree, *Leading Without Power* (San Francisco: Jossey-Bass, Inc., 1997) 138-139.
2. Zig Ziglar, *Breaking Through to the Next Level* (Rapid City, S. Dak.: Honor Books, 1998) 22.
3. Bob Briner, *More Leadership Lessons of Jesus* (Nashville: Broadman & Holman Publishers, 1998) 39.
4. *The Living Webster Encyclopedic Dictionary of the English Language* (The English Institute of America, 1971) 506.
5. Ibid., 611
6. Bob Briner & Ray Pritchard, *The Leadership of Jesus* (Nashville: Thomas Nelson, 1996) 91.

Chapter Three

1. Dale Carnegie, *How to Win Friends and Influence People* (New York: Pocket Books, 1940) 88.
2. Stewart L. Tubbs & Sylvia Moss, *Human Communication* (New York: McGraw Hill, 1974) 143.
3. *Life Application Study Bible* (Wheaton, Ill.: Tyndale Houe Publishers, 1996) 1986.
4. Tubbs & Moss, *Human Communication,* 145.
5. Ralph Nichols, *Effective Listening Skills* (Washington DC: Communications Development, Inc., 1992) 5.
6. The Pace Group, *Effective Reading Skills* (Farmington Hills, Mich.: 1969) 79.
7. Max Depree, *Leadership Is an Art* (New York: Dell Publishing, 1989) viii.
8. B. Eugene Griessman, *Time Tactics of Very Successful People* (New York: McGraw-Hill, 1994) 52.
9. *The Living Webster Encyclopedic Dictionary,* 321.
10. The Pace Group, *Effective Listen Skills* (Farmington Hills, Mich.: Self-published, 1969) 192.
11. DePree, *Leadership Is an Art,* 11.

Chapter Four

1. Malcolm Forbes, *Forbes Book of Business Quotations* (Capitola, Calif.: Black Dog & Leventhal Publishers, 1997) 943.
2. Ibid., 944.

3. Twain in *Forbes Book of Business Quotations,* 916.
4. Blaise Pascal, in *Forbes Book of Business Quotations,* 944.
5. Griessman, *Time Tactics of Very Successful People,* 159.

Chapter Five

1. Fred Smith, *You and Your Network* (Irving, Tex.: Word Books) 139.
2. Ziglar, *Breaking through to the Next Level,* 123.
3. Tubbs & Moss (Source: Albert Meharabian) *Human Communication,* 103.
4. *Prescription for Life* (Grand Rapids, Mich.: Zondervan, 1997) 33.
5. Roger Beale, "Vocal Coaches' Corner—Breathing for Singing 101," *Christian Musician Magazine,* (Crosswalk.com), Music Channel features/item/0,1667,2775,00.html.
6. Clark Carlyle, 38 *Basic Speech Experiences* (Lexington, Ky.: Clark Pubishing, 1960) vii.
7. Griessman, *Time Tactics of Successful People,* 150.
8. Fred Smith, "Making Your Message Memorable," *Leadership Magazine,* Spring 1998, 93.

Chapter Six

1. H.B. Masterman. Source unknown.
2. Dr. Mark Rosekind. Source unknown.
3. "First for Women," *Ideals,* May 1, 2000.

Chapter Seven

1. Source unknown.
2. Ralph Waldo Emerson. Source unknown.
3. John Maxwell, *Developing the Leader within You* (Nashville: Thomas Nelson Publishing, 1993) 25-27.
4. Dandemis. Source unknown.

Chapter Eight

1. Jim Cymbala, *Fresh Wind, Fresh Fire* (Grand Rapids, Mich.: Zondervan, 1997) 49.
2. Bill Pollard, *Soul of the Firm* (New York: Harper Business and Grand Rapids, Mich.: Zondervan, 1996)54.
3. Robert Townsend, *Up the Organization* (New York: Alfred A. Knopf, Inc., 1970) 148-148.
4. *The Living Webster Encyclopedic Dictionary,* 156.
5. DePree, *Leading Without Power,* 116-117.
6. John Maxwell, *The 21 Irrefutable Laws of Leadership* (Nashville: Thomas Nelson, 1998) 143.
7. Bob Briner, *The Leadership Lessons of Jesus* (Nashville: Thomas Nelson, 1996) 91.

8. Ted Engstrom and Alec MacKenzie, *Managing Your Time* (Grand Rapids, Mich: Zondervan, 1967) 125.
9. Ziglar, *Breaking Through to the Next Level*, 22.
10. Mike Murdock, *Leadership Secrets of Jesus* (Tulsa, Okla.: Honor Books, 1996) 81.

Chapter Nine

1. *The NIV Leadershiop Bible*, (Grand Rapids, Mich.: Zondervan Pubishing, 1998) 462.
2. DePree, *Leadership Is an Art*, viii.
3. Kenneth Blanchard, *The Heart of a Leader* (Escondido, Calif.: Honor Books, 1999) 73-75.
4. DePree, *Leading Without Power*, 84-85.
5. Briner, *The Leadership Lessons of Jesus,* 57.
6. James O'Toole, in DePree, *Leadership Is an Art*, xx.
7. DePree, *Leading Without Power*, 84-85.
8. Maxwell, *The 21 Irrefutable Laws of Leadership*, 189.
9. DuPree, *Leadership Is an Art*, 11.
10. Sylvia Nash, *Inspirational Management* (Chicago: Moody Press, 1992) 113.
11. From Lao-tzu as quoted by Townsend, *Up the Organization*, 99.
12. Bob Briner & Ray Pritchard, *More Leadership Lessons of Jesus*, 128.

Chapter Ten

1. Murdock, *Leadership Secrets of Jesus*, 138.
2. Julie Baker, "Let the Dream Begin" (Delaware Water Gap, Penn.: Shawnee Press, 2000) 18327.
3. Hyrum Smith, *The 10 Natural Laws of Successful Time and Life Management* (New York: Warner Books, 1994) 79.
4. Douglas, *Success Secrets*, 107.
5. Attributed to Alexander Graham Bell. Source unknown.
6. January 5, 2000, Madeline Manning Mims in Tulsa, Oklahoma.
7. This prayer is based upon the promises and principles outlined in Psalm 20:4: "May he give you the desires of your heart and make all of your plans succeed," Proverbs 16:9: "In his heart a man plans his course, but the Lord determines his steps," and Proverbs 16:3: "Commit to the Lord whatever you do, and your plans will succeed."

Chapter Eleven

1. Russel Conwell, *Acres of Diamonds* (Kansas City: Hallmark Editions, 1968).
2. *Diamonds: Facts and Fallacies* (Las Vegas: American Gem Society, 1991) 8.

Reasonable care has been taken to trace ownership of the material quoted in this book and to obtain permission to use copyrighted materials when necessary.

Bibliography

Allison, Joseph D. *Setting Goals that Count*. Grand Rapids, Mich.: Zonder van Corporation, 1985.

Aslett, Don. *Is There Life After Housework?* Cincinnati, Ohio: Writer's Digest Books, 1981.

Baker, Julie. "Let the Dream Begin." Delaware Water Gap, Penn.: Shawnee Press, 2000.

Beckwith, Harry. *Selling the Invisible*. New York: Warner Books, 1997.

Blanchard, Ken. *The Heart of a Leader*. Escondido, Calif.: Honor Books, 1999.

Blanchard, Kenneth, and Spencer Johnson. *The One Minute Manager*. New York: William Morrow and Company, Inc., 1982.

Briner, Bob. *Business Basics from the Bible* (formerly *Squeeze Play*). Grand Rapids, Mich.: Zondervan Publishing, 1994.

Briner, Bob. *The Leadership Lessons of Jesus*. Nashville, Tenn.: Thomas Nelson, 1996.

Briner, Bob & Pritchard, Ray. *The Leadership Lessons of Jesus: A Timeless Model for Today's Leaders*. Nashville, Tenn.: Broadman & Holman Publishers, 1997.

Briner, Bob. *The Management Methods of Jesus*. Nashville, Tenn.: Thomas Nelson, 1996.

Briner, Bob and Ray Pritchard, *More Leadership Lessons of Jesus*. Nashville, Tenn.: Broadman & Holman Publishers, 1998.

Brown, Patricia D. *Learning to Lead from Your Spiritual Center*. Nashville, Tenn.: Abingdon Press, 1996.

Carnegie, Dale. *How to Win Friends and Influence People*. New York: Simon and Schuster, 1936.

Charlesworth, Edward A., and Ronald G. Nathan, *Stress Management, A Comprehensive Guide to Wellness*. New York: Ballantine Books, 1982.

Christian, Charles W. "10 Rules for Respect." *Leadership Magazine*, Summer, 1999.

Conwell, Russell, and William R. Webb, eds. *Acres of Diamonds*. Kansas City, Mo.: Hallmark Cards, 1968.

Covey, Stephen R. *The Seven Habits of Highly Effective People, Restoring the Character Ethic*. New York: Simon and Schuster, 1990.

Dayton, Edward R. *Tools for Time Management*. Grand Rapids, Mich.: Zondervan Publishing, 1974.

DePree, Max. *Leadership Is An Art*, New York: Dell Publishing, 1989.

DePree, Max. *Leadership Jazz*, New York: Doubleday, 1992.

DePree, Max. *Leading Without Power*, Holland, Mich.: Shepherd Foundation, 1997.

DeVos, Dick. *Rediscovering American Values*. New York: Dutton of The Penguin Books, 1997.

Diamonds: Facts and Fallacies. Las Vegas, Nev.: American Gem Society, 1991.

Douglas, Merrill. *Success Secrets*. Tulsa, Okla.: Honor Books, 1984.

Eims, LeRoy. *Be the Leader You Were Meant to Be*. Colorado Springs, Colo.: Cook Communications, 1975, 1996.

Engstrom, Ted W. and R. Alec Mackenzie. *Managing Your Time: Practical Guidelines on the Effective Use of Time*. Grand Rapids, Mich.: Zondervan Books, 1967.

Flesch, Rudolf. *Say What You Mean*. New York: Harper and Row Publishers, 1972.

Gray, Alice, Steve Stephens, and John Van Diest. *Lists to Live By*. Sisters, Ore.: Multnomah Publishers, 1999.

Griessman, B. Eugene. *Time Tactics of Very Successful People*, New York: Mc-Graw-Hill, 1994.

Hower, Stephen D. *Sharpening the Sword; A Call to Strong and Courageous Leadership*. Saint Louis: Concordia Publishing House, 1996.

Johnson, Jon. *Christian Excellence*. Grand Rapids, Mich.: Baker Book House, 1985.

Jones, Laurie Beth. *Jesus, CEO: Using Ancient Wisdom for Visionary Leadership*. New York: Hyperion, 1995.

Koch, Richard. *The 80/20 Principle*. New York: Doubleday, 1998.

Life Application Study Bible. Wheaton, Ill.: Tyndale House Publishers, 1996.

Mallory, Sue. "Want-to, Can-do Workers." *Leadership Magazine*, Winter, 1999.

Marple, Joy, Senior Editor. *Prescriptions for Life*, Grand Rapids, Mich.: Zondervan Publishing, 1997.

Marriot, J.W. Jr., and Kathi Ann Brown. *The Spirit To Serve, Marriott's Way*. New York: HarperBusiness, 1997.

Maxwell, John C. *The 21 Irrefutable Laws of Leadership*. Nashville, Tenn.: Thomas Nelson Publishers, 1998.

Maxwell, John C. *Developing the Leader Within You*. Nashville, Tenn.: Thomas Nelson Publishers, 1993.

Meijer, Fred. *Just Call Me Fred*. Grand Rapids, Mich.: Meijer, Inc., 1998.

Murdock, Mike. *Leadership Secrets of Jesus*. Tulsa, Okla.: Honor Books, 1996.

Murphy, Emmett. *Leadership I.Q.* New York: John Wiley & Sons, Inc., 1996.

Nash, Sylvia. *Inspirational Management*. Chicago: Moody Press, 1992.

Peale, Norman Vincent. *The Power of Positive Thinking*. Pawling, New York: Center for Positive Thinking, 1967.

Peter, Laurence and Raymond Hull. *The Peter Principle*. New York: William Morrow and Company, 1969.

Peters, Thomas J. and Robert H. Waterman. Jr. *In Search of Excellence*. New York: Warner Books, 1982.

Phillips, Donald T. *Lincoln on Leadership*. New York: Warner Books, 1992.

Pollard, C. William. *The Soul of the Firm*. Grand Rapids, Mich.: Harper Business and Zondervan Publishing House, 1996.

Richman, Eugene, and Arvinder Brara, *Practical Guide to Managing People*. West Nyack, New York: Parker Publishing Company, 1975.

Rinehart, Stacy T., *Upside Down, The Paradox of Servant Leadership*. Colorado Springs, Colo.: NavPress, 1998.

Sala, Harold, *Unlocking Your Potential*. Vision House, 1996.

Schlenger, Sunny, and Roberta Roesch, *How to Be Organized in Spite of Yourself, Time and Space Management that Works with Your Personal Style*. New York: The Penguin Group, 1990.

Schwartz, David Joseph. *The Magic of Thinking Big*. New York: Simon and Schuster, 1987.

Sherman, Doub, and William Hendricks. *How to Balance Competing Time Demands*. Colorado Springs, Colo.: NavPress, 1989.

Smith, Fred. "Making Your Message Memorable," *Leadership Magazine*, Spring, 1998.

Smith, Fred. *You and Your Network*. Waco, Tex.: Word Books, 1994.

Smith, Hyrum W. *The 10 Natural Laws of Successful Time and Life Management, Proven Strategies for Increased Productivity and Inner Peace*. New York: Warner Books, 1994.

Townsend, Robert. *Up the Organization*. New York: Alfred A. Knopf, Inc., 1970.

Tubbs, Stewart L., and Sylvia Moss. *Human Communication*. New York: Mc-Graw-Hill, 1994.

Van Crouch Communications. *Dare To Succeed*. Wheaton, Ill.: Honor Books, 1994.

Yager, Dexter. *Dynamic People Skills*. InterNET Services Co., USA, 1997.

Ziglar, Zig. *Breaking Through to the Next Level*. Tulsa, Okla.: Honor Books, 1998.

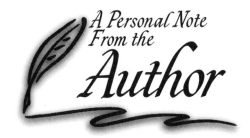
A Personal Note From the **Author**

Heart:

When I was eight and in third grade, I conjured up a daydream where my class was in the gymnasium preparing for a production. Guess who was barking out orders, pointing out where to put chairs and set the stage, and trying to convince the shy ones that they could do this? Well, I guess the only thing that has changed for me is that it has become more than a daydream and I'm much older now!

Each of us as women has the ability to encourage, motivate, and inspire. I know that you possess deep within you God-given resources that have as yet gone untapped. Girl friend, allow God to unlock that door and open a whole new exciting pathway of service to our Lord and Master!

Soul:

Matthew 20:28 reminds us that Jesus "did not come to be served, but to serve." Poor leadership takes away from the organization—as if it exists to serve her; effective leadership exists to build up, encourage, and, yes, serve. You possess God-given talents and characteristics that are yours to give away to those who are in need of your abilities.

Mind:

I highly recommend Carol Kent's *Speak Up with Confidence* book and seminars (speakupspeakerservices.com) and Florence Littauer's CLASS seminars and books on communication skills (714-888-8665).

TimeOut for Women! also provides leadership training that co-incides with the topics covered in *A Pebble in the Pond*. Current two-hour seminar topics include "Which Leadership Style Is for You," "How Jesus Handled Stress," "Time Management Skills," and "The Art of Presenting." New topics are added on a continuing basis. Call 616-676-1646 for booking information or e-mail at timeout598@aol.com. Plus, I'm always happy to provide a full concert or even a few musical specials if I'm your trainer!

Strength:

Since I've written this book, my staff will often look at me and ask, "Now, tell me again what that chapter on stress says about over-commitment? Are you spending enough time in prayer? Aren't you the one who wrote something about delegating?" They have made me accountable to walk what I've talked!

For this reason, I recommend that you read this book with a friend so that you too (two!) can make each other accountable. It's easy for us to get so busy that our activity does not under-score our value system. Placing ourselves under the scrutiny of another often keeps us aware of staying true to our priorities.

Use this book now as a reference tool that you can look to for reminders on how to be the most effective ripple in your pond! Blessings, dear sister!

Dear Heavenly Father,
please awaken within my sister those talents and strengths
that You have given just to her. Lord, provide an excitement
within her to give these gifts away to serve those around
her and to build up Your Kingdom. We dedicate her
and her strengths to You and ask that You provide
ample opportunity for her to serve You and
those around her. Amen.

Julie Baker

♦ *Time Out For Prayer* — First in a series of Time Out For Women books, this devotional focuses on women's specific needs and encourages them to develop more meaningful and consistent prayer lives. Through a combination of devotional thoughts and journaling space, this resource is a personal and powerful tool women will love.

♦ *Time Out for Holiness at Home* — This Bible study covers a host of targeted topics such as developing holiness with God and family members, finances, resisting temptation and more. This unique study brings clarity to an important concept that's often misunderstood and intimidating.

♦ *Time Out for Holiness at Work* — This Bible study for women explores a variety of work-related topics including making wise decisions, learning to delegate, and working with difficult people. Each group study is designed to help women understand what holiness is and how they can attain it through practical application in today's working world.

♦♦ *Author of all 3 books* ♦♦

Julie Baker is the executive producer of the national women's ministry, TimeOut for Women! She is an accomplished songwriter and recording artist. Julie lives in the Grand Rapids, Michigan area with her husband, Paul. They have two adult children, Christy and Steve.

♦ *A Woman's Journey Through Psalms* — This exceptional eight-session study of eight different Psalms helps women learn to study Scripture and apply its truths. Also included is a 10-track music CD from Integrity, Inc. to help women focus in worship on the Psalms as well as memorize Scripture.

♦ *A Woman's Journey Through Ruth* — The book of Ruth reveals that just as Boaz was to Ruth, our Heavenly Father is our Kinsman-Redeemer and that you don't have to be wealthy, famous, or male to be of value.

♦ *A Woman's Journey Through 1 Peter* — Dee Brestin has skillfully intertwined the wilderness journey of 1 Peter with John Bunyan's classic wilderness journey, Pilgrim's Progress. Beautiful illustrations bring to life the great truths of 1 Peter, including the secret of genuine confidence.

♦ *A Woman's Journey Through Luke* — The book of Luke is particularly empathetic to women, emphasizing how the Savior valued them. Come into the home of Elizabeth as Mary arrives, ponder with Mary the amazing events of the Savior's birth, experience the wonder of the sisters of Bethany as they welcome the Savior into their home, and smile as the women surprise the men on Easter morning.

♦ *A Woman's Journey Through Esther* — Controversy abounds in the Book of Esther! Was Vashti wrong to disobey her husband? Did the beauty contest Esther won involve a night in bed with the king? Learn important principles of interpretation to guide not only through Esther, but also through all of Scripture.

♦♦ *Author* ♦♦

Dee Brestin ministers to the hearts of women with her speaking and writing. Besides her many Bible study guides, she is the author of the best-sellers *The Friendships of Women*, *The Friendships of Women Workbook* and *We Are Sisters*. She and her husband, Steve, are the parents of five children and live in Kearney, Nebraska.

• *Storybook Mentors* — Drawing from classic childhood stories, Brenda Waggoner highlights the timeless, biblical truths of our favorite storybook mentors. Readers can revisit the delightful stories and characters and take away fresh insights into what it means to be a disciple of Christ.

• *The Velveteen Woman* — From the pages of the children's classic *The Velveteen Rabbit* comes the universal question that has touched the hearts and minds of millions: "What is Real?" *The Velveteen Woman* is about the transforming love of the Christ Child who came so that we could become real, whole, and connected with our Creator.

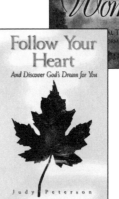

♦♦ *Author of both books* ♦♦
Brenda Waggoner is a licensed counselor practicing in Greenville, Texas. She enjoys music, dancing and reading. She is married to Frank and has two grown sons and a stepson.

• *Follow Your Heart* — Filled with stories of real women, *Follow Your Heart* helps women take practical steps in identifying the person God has called them to be and make progress in achieving their dreams. Going beyond the typical inspirational book, *Follow Your Heart* will enable women to discover their uniqueness and calling and help them find balance in their lives.

♦♦ *Author* ♦♦
Judy Peterson has a business background and now writes and speaks across the country to help women. She is married and has two grown children. The Petersons live in New England.

♦ *Top 10 Mistakes Leaders Make* – Poor leadership habits spawn new generations of poor leaders. Or, they create enough discomfort that the leader figures out how to do it right. This book is for men and women in leadership with little or no formal training. Hans Finzel describes the ten most common leadership blunders. Includes case studies and biblical principles on positive leadership.

♦♦ *Author* ♦♦

Hans Finzel is Executive Director of CBInternational, a church-planting and leadership training ministry currently operating in over 60 countries worldwide. Prior to that, he served as a pastor in Long Beach, California, and spent a decade in Vienna, Austria, as a trainer and administrator for CBInternational in Eastern Europe. Hans and his wife, Donna, are the parents of four children and live in Highlands Ranch, Colorado.

♦ *Engraved On Your Heart* – People have come up with a host of formulas for life. But all of these formulas pale next to the timeless wisdom contained in God's original set of operating instructions. Those directions are found in the Bible and they are called the Ten Commandments. This devotional/Bible study is designed to show you the Ten Commandments in action. You'll discover the lasting truth behind these laws and gain practical help applying these principles effectively in your life.

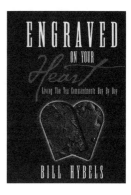

♦♦ *Author* ♦♦

Bill Hybels is the Senior Pastor at Willow Creek Community Church in South Barrington, Illinois. Bill is a husband, father, speaker, consultant, author and serves as Chairman of the Board of the Willow Creek Association.